ORDINARY PEOPLE

By

DR. GARFIELD GREENE

Dedication

This book is dedicated to: My mom and Dad, Mr. Clark Greene, and Mrs. Bertha Greene, to my daughter and grandson Yvette and Nathaniel Phelps, My Wife Deaconess Margie Greene, and my Cousin, Myra (Neicy) DeShields-Moulton.

Acknowledgments

I am grateful to God for the inspiration and opportunity to write. To those who have graciously and freely contributed through interviews. To Dawn Ressler, my editor and Encourager, and to fellow United Methodist Clergy and church members, as well as to family members and friends who have been so supportive of this project.

Ms. Jo Ellen Lofton as a family friend and Great Source of Inspiration.

Introduction

ORDER MY STEPS in thy word, and let not iniquity have rule over me[1].

For a long time now, I have known that God has been guiding my steps and giving direction in my life. But I have often chosen to go my own way and I refused to acknowledge God's voice. I often chose to ignore God's prodding and admonition. All the while, however, I knew that it was for my own good, for the good of the world about me, and for God's glory that God kept me close to the straight and narrow. I walked in what I thought was the proper, moral, and honest path of life; but not strictly so. I usually treated people the way I wanted to be treated, as long as it did not require me to change. Although I knew about God, and had a basic understanding of right and wrong I was really self-centered, and concerned chiefly with my own interests and well-being. Guided by my own faulty logic I found myself in a state of confusion and depression. I knew that God had attempted on several instances to get through to me, but I had chosen to turn a deaf ear to various divine messages.

---

[1]Psalm 119;133 KJV Holy Bible

Experience has taught me, however, that when I strive to follow the Lord's guidance life makes much more sense. In other words, life is a puzzle with a missing piece when I try to do things my way. The Lord is that missing puzzle piece. Although it was not clear to me at first what the Lord wanted me to do, I discovered in due time that I could never be successful in any endeavor when I tried to face life on my own. I had also discovered, in due time, that when I listen to the Lord, things just seem to fall into place.

I have learned that when my plans are God's plans, my plans work. In reality it is God who is in charge. I completely acknowledge my deep need for the Lord in every aspect of my life.

There always seem to be areas in our lives where it is difficult to let God in. God always seems to be welcome in our quiet time, in our times of sacred devotion, and during worship services. God is also welcome at weddings; at least during the time when the vows are taken. Of course we find it easy to welcome and acknowledge God's presence in time of great need or crisis or tragedy. I have become acutely aware, however, that we need God in every part of our lives. Our plans, our thoughts, and our smallest and our greatest decisions are incomplete without God's guidance. If there is a time when God is not welcome in any activity that we are involved in we are walking in the wrong path, and we need to make an immediate and definite change. Sometimes we are quite comfortable walking in the wrong path, and we are reluctant to change. My father, in my opinion, was a man of few words when it came to giving me and my sibling's advice; so we tended to remember some of what he said. I did recall hearing him say that a wise man would change, but that a fool would never change. That saying, remaining indelibly in my mind has helped me to abandon my ways and to endeavor to follow the Lord.

One of my favorite hymns expresses the need that I have for the Lord. It is believed to have been inspired by Psalm 63, verse 1. It is believed that Annie S. Hawks wrote the words to that great hymn around 1850 and that Robert Lowery set the words to music and added the refrain in 1872. According to Mrs. Hawks it was when she was 37 years old, and busy with her duties as a young wife and mother that the thoughts and words came to her. It was all of a sudden that she became so filled with a sense of nearness to the Lord that, she wondered how anyone could live without him either in joy or in pain.

I Need Thee every hour came into her mind and took full possession of her. Years later in a time of loss, those words held for her great comforting power.[2]

I need thee every hour our most gracious lord, no tender voice like mine can peace afford.

I need thee every hour, stay thou nearby, temptations lose their power when thou art nigh.

I need thee every hour, in joy or pain, come quickly and abide, or life is the vain.

I need thee every hour, teach me thy will, and they rich promises in me fulfill.

I need thee every hour, most Holy one, O make me thine indeed, thou blessed Son.

I need thee, Oh I need thee; every hour I need thee. Oh bless me now, my Savior, I come to thee.

For many years that hymn has been, for me, a great source of inspiration and strength. I have always loved music. Singing and praying have been a part of my devotional life as far back as I can remember. My private prayers are often interrupted by a burst of singing hymns like "I Need Thee Every Hour." In fact, that hymn to me is a prayer. It expresses my total dependence on the divine presence of Jesus Christ in every part of my life.

As a child I had experiences that led me to believe that someday I would become a preacher. At the age of 11, for example, I remember one night having a dream that was as clear to me as if I had been wide awake. In that dream I remember that I was speaking from the pulpit to a group of people who were seated in my home church. When I awoke I could not remember what I had been saying; only that the

---

[2] I need thee Every hour Annie S Hawk and Robert Lowry

words were very powerful, and that the people were visibly moved.

My home church was First Baptist Church located on Alice Ann Street in Bel Air, Maryland. The building still remains in the same location but the name has changed. It is now New Hope Baptist Church.

I remember that the church was a very scary place if you were there alone at night. You needed someone there with you; almost anyone who was friendly would do. In the winter time, after the heat was turned on the church became very noisy. As the hot water from the boiler flowed through the pipes it caused great creaking and banging sounds.

I used to have dreams about going into the church, singing on the choir, and daring to go down into the cellar where the giant boiler was and where the pipes that fed the radiators and filled and emptied the baptismal pool were located. Eventually I did go down there a few times to turn on the water for the pool in preparation for baptisms. The place was pitch dark, and musty and the light switch was hard to find. I tell you, it was enough to cause a twelve-year-old boy to get serious about praying.

The church cellar was not one of my favorite places. The truth is that I was very much afraid when I went there alone; but I was not afraid enough to refuse to go. I did like to go to church though. It was there that I first learned to play the piano before I had ever studied music.

I actually taught myself to play. I used to go to the sanctuary alone and try to pick out tunes and make sensible harmonic sounds. There was only one piano in the church. It was an old upright Baldwin piano that had the most beautiful sound that I ever heard.

When I would go there alone it was as if I had found buried treasure. In the summer the church was hot, and in the winter the church was cold because the congregation could not afford to keep the church warm except during services. However, neither the heat nor the cold kept me from being in the church when I could play the piano. I had an ear for music, and there were few things in life that delighted me as much as making music on an instrument.

Although I did not have the opportunity to take music lessons at that time, over the years I have studied piano, organ, guitar, trumpet and cello. When I was thirteen I started taking piano lessons from my uncle, Mr. Lueray Norris. He was my mother's youngest brother who taught piano and organ for a living. I learned a lot from him, although I was not able to continue traveling to Baltimore where he had his studio. Later on, after becoming an adult I studied from other teachers.

My most recent teachers with whom I studied Classical music were Mrs. Elma Adams from Westminster Choir College in Princeton, New Jersey; and Mrs. Martha Mihich in Atlantic City, New Jersey. Mrs. Mihich was a retired concert pianist whose teacher had been taught by Franz List. In addition, I have studied Musical Composition with Dr. Robert Lau, in Camp Hill, Pennsylvania. Dr. Lau has published over 200 musical works including over 150 Choral and Organ works published by the leading music publishing companies in the United States. I am currently studying Cello with Mrs. Dina Slechta of East Petersburg, Pa. Music excites me now every bit as much as it did sitting at that old Baldwin Upright.

For me, and I imagine for many others, the church scene was about the only opportunity for social interaction with my peers outside of school. The First Baptist Church played a major role in my emotional and spiritual formation. It was there that I first learned something about the power of the words in the Bible. It was there that I first felt the excitement, fervor and power of Christian worship in the African American church. At that time, I had few worship experiences in White churches. For me those few experiences seemed authentic, sincere, spiritual and polite, but lacked the energy that I was used to at First Baptist. Nearly every time I walked into the narthex at First Baptist I experienced a warm tingling feeling like a very low electrical current flowing through my body. I have felt that same experience in only a few churches over the years.

Although I tried to find a psychological reason for that experience I have been unsuccessful. Therefore, I have concluded that it was, for me, an authentic example of the almost tangible presences of God in my life. It was the Comforter; the Holy Spirit. To this day I find a real comfort and peace in Christian church sanctuaries.

As I recall, the First Baptist Church Sanctuary had beautiful colored-glass windows. At that time, it seemed to me that the ceiling was very high. At our church the services always lasted for at least two hours, and nobody seemed to mind. Sometimes during the uninteresting phases of the service I used to look up and try to count the ceiling tiles, but I was never successful. To the right, as you sat facing the pulpit there was a section of four shorter benches that faced the pulpit from the side. There the Deacons of the church would sit throughout every service. From that section of the church lively fervent prayers would come forth.

I distinctly remember the prayers of Deacon Robert Carrington. When Deacon Bob would get down on one knee and call upon the Lord he would intone a prayer that would last for at least 15 to 20 minutes. He would begin by thanking God for another day that he had never seen before, and for allowing him to wake up in "time and not eternity." He was thanking God that his "cover was not his winding sheet and his bed was not his cooling board." He would go on to thank the Almighty God that "the blood was still running warm in his veins." It was clear that Deacon Bob was glad to be alive! He would pray for everyone he knew, for those who knew him and many people that he only knew of. He would pray for the "widows and fatherless children all over the land and country," and "everyone who was standing in the need of prayer." When Deacon Bob came down to the end of his prayer Deacon Jones would rise and begin to pray, "Father I stretch my hands to thee, no other help I know—" Sometimes his prayer was even longer, but those men seemed quite sincere. Although much of what they said in their prayers was often repeated in every prayer there seemed to be fervent communication with God.

The church benches were hard, on Sundays the services were quite long, and I always got hungry long before the benediction. Amazingly, I got used to the long prayers and the lengthy services, but I never adjusted to having to wait for such a long time before the next meal. After a good number of years had passed I did preach at The First Baptist Church in Bel Air. I have been preaching the gospel now for over 30 years.

I remember another dream that came to me when I was in my 20's. I remember that dream today as if it were yesterday. I saw myself in a kneeling position, reaching down and picking up dark mud from below. The mud would slip through my fingers and there would remain only diamonds and pearls and other precious jewels that were still partially covered with thick black dirt. I would hand those stones to someone who was positioned above me, and then reached down to gather up more dirt. In the dream the place where I was working was rather dark. My working environment was not very pleasant but I was extremely excited about what I was doing. In that dream I did not recall having any help except from the person above me whom I could almost touch.

At the time, the dream puzzled me to the extent that I decided to seek an interpretation. There have always been members of ethnic communities who were trusted implicitly and were seen as prophets, or special resource people. In their effort to understand some of life's mysteries, what was understood as blessings, curses, good luck, bad luck, etc. people have always sought out individuals whom they believed had the ability to predict and, in some cases to help them to control their future and destiny. Unfortunately, the vast majority of those who claiming to have the ability to predict or change one's future have always been frauds. Such frauds have always made a great deal of money by playing on the emotions, the fears, and the superstitions of people who are weak, unsure of themselves, and are living with feelings of failure and hopelessness.

Ms. Lillian Thompson, however, was a very wise elderly Christian woman who was a supportive member of a legitimate church in the community. Ms. Thompson seemed to have a special ability to council people who were troubled. She was a kind and altruistic person who opened her hand and her home to the poor. Many of the local people, and even people from other states confided in her to help them find answers to their spiritual problems. Some of my family members trusted her as well. The first time I witnessed what I truly believe was a faith healing I was in Mrs. Lillian's waiting room. There were about 10 people waiting to see her. After we had sat there for about 10 minutes Ms. Lillian came into the room and went over to a woman who was sitting in a wheelchair and holding two crutches. She was in obvious pain and could not walk on her own. After saying a powerful prayer of faith, Mrs. Thompson took the woman by her hand and told her to get up. Helping herself with the crutches the woman carefully lifted herself from the chair. As the woman began to follow Ms. Lillian, she told her to put down the crutches. Following her directions, the woman followed her as she walked about the room praising God and waving her arms freely above her head. It was not long before the woman who had been healed folded up her wheelchair and walked perfectly out of the house. What I saw was a real healing. I knew it had not been staged because I had seen the pain in the woman's face.

I went to Ms. Lillian one day and told her about the dream I had about the valuable jewels. She told me that the jewels I was gathering from the dirt were precious souls, and that I was giving them to the Lord who would clean them up and use them in his service. Over the past 30 years I have witnessed many conversions that happened, either through my preaching, witnessing or through personal evangelism. I have often thought about that dream and Ms., Lillian's interpretation. Over the years I have prayed that I might faithfully carry out that assignment. There is also a passage of scripture that has become more meaningful to me since I have pondered the dream.

"I waited patiently for the Lord to help me: and he turned to me and heard me cry. He lifted me out of the pit of despair, and out of the mud and mire. He set my feet on the solid ground as steadied me as I walked along."[3]

When I was growing up some of the older people in my

---

[3]Psalm 40 verses 1 and 2.

community said they were sure that I had some kind of special calling. Others simply said they thought I had what they called a "leaning toward religion." I knew that God had special work for me to do, but I was at a loss as to what that work was. Early on, I was sure that I had a special relationship with God, although I almost never talked to anyone about it. In all my personal endeavors, experiences and especially my problems, I always considered God. I wondered where God was in those matters. I wondered if God was pleased or displeased with me. I would always hope that God would forgive me for making foolish mistakes. I knew that God was good, and I knew right from wrong.

One evening I had an interesting conversation with Mr. Joe Evans. Everyone in town knew Mr. Joe. He was a local man who worked hard at odd jobs but spent most of his money on alcohol. I told Mr. Joe that I believed God was with us and would protect us if we believed in him. He said he believed in God and prayed as well, but he thought he needed a little extra help. He said that was why he carried his switchblade with him. His reasoning sounded logical, but I knew he was wrong. The preacher had told us that God would fight our battles and I believed that; I still do. I have also learned that Jesus called his disciples and said, "Follow me."

I know now that Jesus still calls us to be his disciples and to follow him. And when He calls us, it is not a temporary summons. We are to follow Him for the rest of our days. I have heard that call, and I am determined to walk in the straight and narrow path as long as I live.

Involuntary military servitude, or conscription came to an end in this country when the United States military changed to an all-volunteer military force. The Selective Service system still remains in place, however, and can be reactivated if the situation warrants it. Men who are between the ages of 18 and 25 are required to register so that the draft can be resumed if it is needed. Since I was of draft age, and did not want to be drafted into a branch of service that was not of my choosing, I decided to visit my local Air Force Recruiter. He did a very good job of convincing me that the United States Air Force was just where I belonged, and where I wanted to be. I did join the Air Force, and was honorably discharged, but I discovered early on that I was not suited for a military career. I did derive some particular benefits from being in the Service.

Early on I understood that as an American Citizen I had a military duty to perform in service to my country. I felt a sense of pride that I was even eligible to serve. I had to show proof that I had completed High School, pass a physical test, and a written exam. As an American Airman I almost always felt respected, and sometimes envied. Although I have been a civilian for many years now I have never lost the pride that I found as a member of the United States Air Force.

The military afforded me my first opportunity to travel more than 50 miles from home. It gave me my first airplane ride, and many other new experiences. I learned how to take responsibility, and the value of teamwork and organization. You can learn from other people's experience. You can always do more than you think you can. That spirit of determination did not leave me when I left the Air Force. I approach tasks and responsibilities as a civilian with a new discipline that I acquired in boot camp.

Thanks to my military experience I have a good measure of self-discipline and self-confidence. One of the benefits of active military service in the United States is the right to receive financial support for educational pursuits. With the help of the GI Bill I was able to earn a Bachelor's Degree in French, and a Master's Degree in Clinical Social Work.

Military service changes people in many ways; some negative, and some positive. I think most of us are able to lead, and to follow directions. We can usually work with many different types of people. We are usually good at working under pressure, and getting the job done. Because of the regimented military systems, we are able conform to rules and regulations. I am thankful for my military experience, and I am thoroughly convinced that it has made a better person.

When I left Bel Air, Maryland to go to college at Morgan State College, which is now Morgan State University, in Baltimore, I knew that the hand of God was guiding me. When

I enrolled at the University of Maryland School of Social Work and Community Planning, I knew that God was leading me. When I became a Lay Speaker, completing the Basic Course at the United Methodist Church in Perry Hall, Maryland in the 70s it was clear to me that God had special plans for my life, and becoming a Lay Speaker was a vital step in realizing those plans.

During the early stages of the Methodist Church there were not sufficient numbers of clergymen available. So, in order to help fill the void, people who were not ordained were permitted to assume positions of leadership in Methodist churches in many communities. Clergymen covered the long circuits, preaching and administering the sacraments which for Methodists are baptism and The Lord's Supper. There were often long periods when the church members did not have the convenience of a clergyman. In the meantime, persons of strong Christian conviction and commitment led the services. Those faithful leaders either did not want to be ordained, or they did not have the time to go through the process of preparation and ordination.

Lay speakers led worship, preached, taught, led small groups, cared for the sick, and held the members accountable to live as Methodist Christians. Today, people from all walks of life become lay speakers. They represent many cultural and ethnic groups. They are women and men, boys and girls and retirees. Today they are busy leading Bible studies, caring for the needs of the community of faith, the programs of the church, and filling the pulpit when clergy are not available.

When I was working at the Perry Point Veterans Administration Hospital as a Psychiatric Social Worker, God spoke to me through a Methodist Chaplain there. Dr. John Richardson had heard that I had been doing some preaching in local churches and suggested that I should go to the Seminary and become theologically and academically prepared for ordination. The prospect of becoming ordained excited me.

At the time I had not become personally acquainted with any theological schools, and did not know where to begin. Since Chaplain Richardson was an alumnus of the Princeton

Theological Seminary he suggested that I might give some consideration to begin there. He even took the time to accompany me on a visit to Princeton, introduced me to some members of the faculty, and helped me to become familiar with the entry procedures. I am very grateful for his urging. Following his advice, I did attend Princeton Seminary, and graduated with a Master of Divinity degree. After working for a few years as a full-time United Methodist Pastor, God communicated to me that I should pursue doctoral studies. I attended Wesley Theological Seminary in Washington, DC and was awarded a Doctor of Ministry degree.

God has spoken to me again very clearly since then. When I say that God speaks to me, I do not mean that I hear an audible voice from heaven, or from anywhere else. I mean that something within me, but from beyond me, takes the reins of my conscience, and moves me to listen and obey. This time I was urged by the same divine authority to write a book about how God uses ordinary people to accomplish his purposes in the world. I was to tell true stories about a few ordinary people who intimately touched my life or the lives of others; how they experienced God in their lives, and how God used them to bring glory to himself. I was to include examples where people trusted God alone for salvation, protection, guidance and sustenance. I would also point out how such people's trust helped move others to faith. I was to be clear about the reality that God's regular people invariably faced challenges, conflicts, frustrations, pain and sorrows, but also joys and miracles. Whenever it was possible, I would speak personally with God's ordinary people about their personal lives under the guidance of God, and the Lordship of Jesus Christ. In addition, I would rely on impressions left by God's people on the world, and on all of those who knew them. I would draw on Old and New Testament Scriptures for Biblical and Theological support.

It is my hope that this publication will help enlighten and encourage people who know little or nothing about the practical application of the Christian faith. I hope through this book to encourage and strengthen the Saints of the Lord who have accepted the claims of the Risen Christ and are living examples of those who have been born from above. Please be assured that if you read this book, you will step into the lives of some very special but ordinary people. It is my sincere hope and prayer that my esteemed readers will be informed, encouraged and blessed.

What is an ordinary person? The word ordinary can be defined as plain, average, regular, or undistinguished. But what is ordinary to me might be totally different from what is ordinary to you. The reader must determine the meaning of ordinary. For me, an ordinary person is one with whom I can readily identify, to whom I can relate, and whose story connects with my story at important points. Some of the people the reader will meet may not be famous, or maybe not even successful by the standards of modern society. They may be merely Christian believers. It is not this author's intent to praise or celebrate the accomplishments of any individual, although some successes that have come through persistent faith, sacrifice and dedication will be acknowledged. My goal is to glorify God in the stories of the lives of ordinary Christians.

So that the reader may understand the author as an average, unexceptional person, I am including a brief autobiographical sketch. While it is not complete in terms of detailed personal information, it does include some important personal experiences that I wish to share.

My Beginnings

"I REMEMBER THE day when the kids came to school saying, Mrs. Bertha Greene had a baby boy." I heard those words at the Salem United Methodist Church in Pleasantville, New Jersey. It was a church member who spoke them to me. The person speaking was a semi-retired school teacher whose brother had a married relative on my father's side of the family. She informed her new pastor that she had knowledge of him and his family. Thelma Cordery has been a very warm and faithful support to me and my wife, Margie, for a lot of years. Mrs. Cordery, who later became Mrs. Hall for many years has never failed to send beautiful greeting cards on any occasion. I believe she had the most beautiful penmanship that I have ever seen. It reminded me of my mother who always took the time to find beautiful cards to send to people she cared about. Whenever mother had the opportunity, she would spend a little time in the local drug store, or the local stationary store, looking for the most beautiful cards she could find. She would buy the cards and put them aside for some special occasion in someone's life.

    I was born in Bel Air, Maryland. Bel Air is the county seat of Harford County, located on United States Route One, about 24 miles north of Baltimore city. The town was different when I was born there over 70 years ago. By now it has grown into a major shopping town with a population of some 10,080 residents[1]. Today shoppers can find Sears, several other large stores, more than one major mall and a hospital just outside of town.

    When I was a boy growing up in Bel Air, the nearest hospital was 30 miles away. There were only two practicing medical doctors in Bel Air at the time. I was born at home: the

---

[1] According to the 2000 census information.

doctor came to our house. I don't know if he arrived before or after I was born, only that he was there.

Bernice

I ASKED MY sister, Bernice, to share something about her experience as a young girl growing up in Bel Air. Bernice was quite a bit older than I was. In fact, she was nine years older than me. Therefore, as a child growing up, I had never gotten to know very well since her peers were much more mature than mine were. She told me that Mom and Dad had moved to Bel Air from Muddy Creek Forks in York County, Pennsylvania when she was five or six years old. Bernice started school when she was six years old. There were no kindergarten or Head Start programs in existence at that time. Many of the African American women did household work for White families. Those relationships were very positive and the employers seemed to be very caring. In Bernice's own words "It was almost like an extended family. People were thoughtful, caring and kind, but we were socially separated." During the time that she worked for the owners of the Yew Tree Inn in Bel

Air Bernice said that she never experienced any racial problems that she could recall.

Bernice said that everybody knew everybody, and that the money was not good but that there were other benefits. For example, the employees were given clothing and shoes, and they were helped out in other ways.

Speaking about the people that both mother and Bernice worked for, Bernice said that they never made you feel inferior. Black women took care of white babies almost as part of their own family. Our dad, Clark Greene worked in concrete for many years. The work was difficult, and he became quite arthritic as a result, but the money was good. He told us proudly that he had built the first sidewalks in Bel Air. He did not have the money to purchase the property that we lived on. It was purchased for him by his employer, Mr. Charles Lutz, a businessman from New York; and our family paid for it over time.

As a child Bernice said that she cherished the words, "I would not have you ignorant." She said she knew that those words came from the Bible and they gave her a lot of courage. Those words did come from the Bible. In fact, they can be found in 1st Thessalonians 4; 13-14. That passage of scripture actually refers to the Christian hope in the Resurrection of Christ. Although she was not aware of the meaning of those words in the proper biblical context my big sister found in them great strength.

Bernice loved school and was very dedicated. She did the best she could under the limited circumstances. Bernice said, "I did not know then that I was poor. I did not know that there was so much missing. I thought my life was normal because everybody else I knew lived the same way. Mother worked all the time. We had food, but not a great variety of food. I remember walking to school through all kinds of weather. I also remember being glad to get a plate with nuts and candy and oranges for Christmas. That's all we got. There were no toys, unless we made them ourselves. I made my own doll. I read everything I could find, although I had to read by lamp light. One of the first books I read was <u>The Good Earth</u>, written by Pearl Buck. I remember that it taught me a lot about the people of China. The next book I read was <u>Native Son</u>. I always wanted to learn everything I could, and because I did not have the opportunity to travel, I had to learn by reading. I graduated from high school with a perfect attendance for 11 years. I received a certificate for perfect attendance."

After getting married and raising several children, Bernice decided to become a nurse. She attended school and became an LPN and then an RN, passing her State Boards both times on the first attempt.

When I asked Bernice about her belief in God, she was more than willing to talk about it. "I was baptized when I was 12 years old. I knew that God was there for you when nobody else was. God was there when you needed someone to talk to, who would listen and give you some of the things you needed or wanted. I knew I could wish for something or ask for something and receive it. At first I thought I might be talking to myself, but later on, I learned that it was God who was answering my prayers. For example, I always wanted to go to college, but there was no way to get there. When I first went to college, my high school principal provided transportation. I saw that as a blessing from God. I was able to attend the Eastern Shore division of the University of Maryland for two years. I remember that I did not have to take English because I scored so high. I loved football, dramatics club and choir. In college I earned spending money by babysitting for college professors. It made me feel good to be the first in my family to attend college. That was in September of 1946. At that time the schools were segregated."

It should be clear that none of us appreciated the racial inequality that was prevalent during those years, but most African Americans who lived in and around Bel Air accepted it as a way of life for the time being. The older members of our community hoped for a better future in terms of equal rights and opportunities, and the younger generation resisted Jim Crow Laws in any way we could.

Jim Crow laws were state and local laws enforcing racial segregation in the Southern United States. Enacted after the

Reconstruction period, these laws continued in force until 1965. They mandated *de jure* **racial segregation** in all public facilities in states of the former Confederate States of America, starting in 1890 with a "separate but equal" status for African Americans. Conditions for African Americans were consistently inferior and underfunded compared to those available to white Americans. This body of law institutionalized a number of economic, educational, and social disadvantages. *De jure* segregation mainly applied to the Southern states, while Northern segregation was generally *de facto* — patterns of housing segregation enforced by private covenants, bank lending practices, and job discrimination, including discriminatory labor union practices.

Jim Crow laws mandated the segregation of public schools, public places, and public transportation, and the segregation of restrooms, restaurants, and drinking fountains for whites and blacks. The U.S. military was also segregated, as were federal workplaces, initiated in 1913 under President Woodrow Wilson. By requiring candidates to submit photos, his administration practiced racial discrimination in hiring.[2]

As Bernice shared those experiences with me, I suddenly felt closer to her that I ever had before. I thought I had known her before, but after that conversation I felt that I knew her much better.

We lived in a house that sat on a 14-acre lot. My father, Mr. Clark Andrew Greene built the house himself. It wasn't really a large house, but it was home. Back then I knew very little about the amenities enjoyed in modern homes. We got our water from a spring located about 50 yards from the house. I used to have nightmares about going past the spring and being surprised by copperhead snakes. I never saw one, but I knew that they were around. We all knew that they were around. They smelled like cucumbers. Usually, in August, the spring would not produce enough water and we would have to go to the branch, a stream in the valley. That was over sixty years ago, and the streams near Bel Air were not polluted.

---

[2] Information on Jim Crow Laws from Wikipedia.

Sometimes we would get water from our friendly neighbors Mr. and Mrs. Wesley Lakins.

The Friedman's, a very loving African American couple who lived about half a mile away had a well and pump that had to be primed. They were always glad to allow us to get water. About another half mile away there was an ice plant where we paid a nickel for a piece of ice that was almost too big for me to carry. I remember Mr. Jake, the man who worked in the ice plant and waited on us. He was also a friendly person and who seemed somewhat strange because he always talked to himself out loud. But when we greeted him he would respond to us without missing a beat and then resume his conversation with himself. I never knew anything else about Mr. Jake.

We did not have indoor plumbing, and we heated our house by a wood stove. Our house was not located far from the railroad tracks. We used to set our clocks by the morning train. We used to call the train the Mom and Pop. It was the Maryland and Pennsylvania Railroad. As the cross ties became worn, the railroad workers would take them up and lay them in stacks alongside the tracks. The ties were of no more use to the railroad company, but they made very good firewood. We used them although they had been treated with creosote, a chemical preservative that was very harmful if inhaled.

Recently, I discovered that I still have strong emotional connections to trains. On a recent trip to Strasburg, Pennsylvania, Margie and I enjoyed an evening meal, live entertainment and a ride on the historic railroad. The cars had been reconditioned and the ride was absolutely charming. The trip was slow and short, but felt quite authentic. About halfway through the trip, the train stopped. The conductor told a tale about an engine that had gotten stuck up on the Hill and was never able to get down. He said that people called it a ghost train because over the years they could hear it but could not see it. The he said, "Let's listen, we might just hear it." Then we heard a long lonesome train whistle blowing in the distance. It sounded exactly like the Mom and Pop that used to wake me up every morning for most of my childhood years. Just then

Margie said something to me, but I didn't answer. I don't even know what she said. I was hiding my eyes in my hands. I was crying.

Since we did not have electricity, we had to rely on kerosene lamps for light at night. As I recall, our house had only one large room, but it was partitioned off. In all, six of us grew up there. It was Earl, Bernice, Marie, Kathleen, David, and me. Earl was the oldest, and David the youngest. By today's standards I suppose that we might have been classified as poor, but we didn't feel poor. We always had plenty to eat, good clean clothes to wear and we were kept warm. Mother used to get us to help hang the clothes on the line to dry. The clothesline was just a little way from the house. I remember hearing the sheets and towels flapping in the wind. I somehow appreciated the smell of bleached clothes; they just smelled so clean. I always had trouble hanging up clothes because I couldn't get the clothes pins to hold. When it was cold sometimes the clothes would become stiff; not because of the starch, but because they froze on the line.

When it was real cold, we used to take flat irons, wrap them up in towels and put them in our beds near our feet. A flat iron is a nonelectric iron with a flat bottom that was heated and used for the purpose of pressing or ironing clothes. I heard that some people used bricks. I remember that I burned my foot once when I kicked the towel off the iron during the night while I was asleep. It was quite a painful experience. I didn't realize what had happened until the next morning.

Some of my friends, as I recall, were not as well-off as we were. Come to think of it, and I have thought of it before, we had chickens, pigs, rabbits and a garden. That was pretty good I thought. My father said that we could live off the land, and that the only thing that we would have to buy would be salt and pepper and such. He wanted me to stay home and work the land, to be a farmer. I didn't have the talent, the patience or the inclination. But I have always had the utmost respect for the people who produce our food, and especially those who live off the land.

I used to go barefoot during the week in the summer and

just wear shoes on special occasions, such as when we went to Church on Sundays, or when the Carnival came to town. But it scares me when I think about it, the fact that we used to go barefoot so much. I hurt my feet several times when I stepped on something sharp like a nail or broken glass. When that happened to us, Mother made us soak our feet in hot water and Epsom salt, or just plain salt. In a couple of days, we would be just fine. The salt would burn like mad though! The Epsom salt was not as bad, but Mom told us that soaking our feet that way would keep us from getting lockjaw. Lockjaw is a layman's term for tetanus, an infectious disease that can be fatal. It is caused by certain germs that enter the body through wounds. According to a friend who is an RN, one of the symptoms of tetanus is stiffness of voluntary muscles, especially those in the neck and lower jaw.

When we went out from the house, we had to pass by a spring and down a long lane through the woods. In order to get to the main road, we had to walk for about a quarter of a mile. That walk was not bad during the day. The large oak and poplar trees provided protection from the hot sun and from the rain during spring and summer. We did have to watch out for the critters: snakes and pole cats. At night, however, it was a different story. Most of the time it was too dark for us to see where we were going. If we forgot to bring a flashlight or if the moon was not shining, we would just run down the lane using our own radar. We were so used to the path that we could literally find our way in the dark. Now and then we did run into a problem however. I remember one night my younger brother David came in really late and encountered a porcupine. As you can imagine he was quite upset, but that didn't stop him from coming in late at night.

My Brother David

David was always quite the determined young man. He became a Management Consultant before most Americans knew what a Management Consultant was. Since that time God has allowed him to reach many goals that one would have thought were impossible for a young African-American who grew up in the wooded area of Bel Air, Maryland some fifty years ago. Today he is an independent and successful businessman

I remember the first time I paid my own way to the movies. I was 12 years old then, and had gotten a job taking the ashes out of Mrs. Harper's cellar. It was quite a challenge. Her furnace was fueled by coal, and it produced a lot of dusty and dirty ashes. Since I got paid fifty cents, and the movie was thirty-five cents I was able to buy a soda and some Cracker Jacks. At the movie house there were stairs situated on the outside and to the right where African-Americans had to enter. As a youngster I enjoyed the movies tremendously, and went as often as I could with my friends.

Television had been invented, but it had not reached us yet. We did have a battery operated radio. The kids were not allowed to touch it. I remember turning it on once when no one else was around, but I felt guilty about it for quite a while. I can still remember the short hum I heard before I turned it off. We listened to the radio on two occasions: once a day to get the news about the war and on Saturday nights when the Grand Old Opry came on from Nashville, Tennessee. That was a very popular country radio show that continues to play to this day.

When I was little, I thought about God a lot, but usually only when someone in the family passed away. People in Bel Air used to say that God had taken them home. The other time I thought about God was when I got a pain in my stomach from eating green apples-apples that were not yet ready for human consumption. My friends and I would sometimes help ourselves to apples from a neighbor's tree on our way home from school. Of course we had taken the apples without getting the neighbor's permission. I was thoroughly convinced that God was punishing me. In my way of thinking, God was some kind of an angel or spirit who rewarded people when they were good and punished them when they were bad. As I think back on it now, God got the blame for a lot of things that

I did to myself. At that time, I knew very little about the Lord. The truth is that it was the fear of divine retribution that kept me pretty close to the straight and narrow for most of my teen and young adult years.

I had been scared straight early on while attending the First Baptist Church on Aliceanne Street in Bel Air. There used to be a residence on Baltimore Pike that we called The Hall where African American families who had come from North Carolina, South Carolina and Georgia lived. Some of the families attended the First Baptist Church. My family went there too. There were only two churches in Bel Air where African-Americans worshiped at that time. I don't recall having heard that we were not allowed or that we were discouraged from going to any of the churches where the white people went. The churches we went to were the Ames Methodist Church, and the First Baptist Church.

The Methodist Church seemed very formal, but the members took their religion just as seriously as the Baptists. Most of the people who lived in The Hall were very serious about their faith. At church, experience meetings would precede the more formal part of the service. The experience meeting, a practice that was started by the early Methodists, was a time of personal testimony, singing and praising God. Anyone who felt moved by the Spirit could raise a hymn. The individual would simply start to sing a song in a spontaneous manner and the rest of the group would join in. I seem to remember that most people would join in whether they could sing or not. But that never seemed to present a problem. Their desire was to sing and to make a joyful noise unto the Lord, and so they did just that. However, there were some great singers whose voices seemed to reach heaven. None of those people, to my knowledge had ever had any voice lessons, but some sang as if they had. It was truly a moving experience. I used to love to hear Jenny Mae sing. It seemed that she could reach very high notes anytime she wanted to. Without a doubt her voice and singing ability were truly from God! I don't know if Jenny Mae still sings, but I will never forget the wonderful melodious sounds that she produced every time she sang *"Earth has no sorrow that heaven cannot heal.*[3] "I remember hearing Sister Blanche Fuller sing a song that said, "*You can't hide it's no use to try. God's got your number and he knows where you live. Death has a warrant for you*[4]." She would sing that song with such conviction and so convincingly that I didn't think we needed a sermon after that. Strangely enough, one day when I opened the King James Bible, I turned to the 139th Psalm and began to read. As I read, the words of Sister Blanche's song seemed to reverberate in my mind.

---

[3] *Words:* Thomas Moore, *Sacred Songs*, 1816
[4] Lyrics from Death's Got a Warrant. Origins unknown

My Niece Rhonda

SINCE BERNICE'S GRANDDAUGHTER, Rhonda had been influenced by her grandmother, and since Rhonda's was agreeable I thought I would ask her to sit for an interview. She agreed, and what follows is the result of our conversation.

I asked Rhonda what were her earliest notions about God.

"I do not remember when I did not go to church. After all, I am the granddaughter of a preacher. My grandmother, the Reverend Bernice Watkins was an Ordained Baptist Minister. I looked forward to church. I could see my friends there. You see, I had two sets of friends; those at school, and those at church. I only got to see the ones at church once a week, unless we went to VBS (Vacation Bible School), then I would see them for a week. Actually there were times when I would go to VBS all summer. I liked both sets of friends, but my church friends were nicer in general. I had a good feeling about church. I liked to sing on the choir although I am not a singer; not like my mother. People love to hear my mother sing. After church there would be food. That was the best part with the deserts and all.

During my early teens I used to think of things I wanted to do outside the home. When I wanted to do something I would pray for my mother's permission. If I ever did anything wrong my mother would punish me by taking away the things I liked to do. She would not let me go to my Modern Dance class. God didn't punish me. My mother did. Sometimes I feel like God is punishing me now because I always wanted to be married, but I have never been married. God is all powerful, omnipotent, knows all and sees all. God is like a parent that wants the best for you. He allows you to go through some things, then you can appreciate the experience. God doesn't give you bad things to do but it's sort of like the school of hard knocks. God does not turn his back on you. If we are headed down the wrong path God intervenes to show us that there is a better way. These kind of thoughts came to me as an adult, not as a teenager.

As a teenager I accepted the fact that God is real, that we need to pray for forgiveness because we are all sinners. But as long as you believe you will be forgiven.

I have experienced God's forgiveness. I believe, coming through my accident, that was the hand of God. I broke my neck. I was in the emergency room for a long time. I remember my grandmother coming and praying with me. I was scared. I thought I was going to die. I kept asking the doctors, but never got a direct answer. They just said they would do the best that they could. I felt that I needed prayer to come through it. I was in surgery for ten to twelve hours. I am sure that God brought me through it. I could have died, or been paralyzed from the neck down, but I was not. On the Cat Scan you could see that my spinal cord was compressed. The doctor said that there was no way that I should have been saved. The neck is the top of the spinal cord. The spinal cord is responsible for movement. If it is severed, any part of the body below where it is severed would be paralyzed. Mine was broken at C 5, 6 and 7. Mine was similar to a diver's injury, like that of a person who dives into a pool striking their head on the bottom and causing a compression. I had to forgive the person who hit me. They said that I was the cause of the accident, and basically said that I got what I deserved. They had less than $30,000.00 worth of insurance; the minimum allowable by the state. My medical bills were over $100,000.00. The Insurance company wanted me to sue her and take her house, but I did not sue because I did not want to take her home away from her. The Insurance Company settled for the amount that she had. So I forgave her. It was an accident. It was not intentional. She had a negative attitude about it. If I had caused such an accident I would have had a different attitude. The police had determined that she was at fault.

The accident happened on November the 26th, 1996. I had just become an RN in July of 96. I had been able to see the good outcomes versus the bad outcomes; gunshot wounds, seeing those who survive versus those who do not survive. I was very fortunate because some people may not have come out as well as I did. They took a bone from my hip and did a fusion on my neck. I walked with a walker for about six months; I also had a broken ankle from the accident.

My grandmother Bernice was an influence in my becoming a nurse. When we were living on East Preston Street in Baltimore she would come home from work with that white uniform on. I just thought that was the neatest thing around since sliced bread! There was something about that uniform that made me want to be a nurse so that I could also wear a white uniform. At that time, I was between five and six years old. Later on I discovered that I could not stand the sight of blood, but I knew I wanted to be a nurse because I wanted to wear that white uniform. Funny, they don't wear white uniforms much anymore.

I did not want to go to college but my mother forced me to go. At that time, I went for accounting. I did not do well because I didn't want to be there, and after the first year I didn't go back.

After I had my second child I realized that I could no longer work two and three jobs with children. I decided to go to Nursing school because then I would be able to get along working at only one job and not be gone all the time.

I had always hated science. I heard that you had to take a lot of science courses for Nursing. That deterred me. But the desire in me to become nurse, driven by the image of that white uniform helped me to overcome. Interestingly, those courses, the prerequisite science courses, I found interesting. One of the most interesting courses I had was Microbiology because it taught me so much about things that you can't see. It reinforced my faith because you had to look closely at things. Some things you cannot see even though you look for a long time. Faith is believing that something exists although you cannot see it. Some people find Microbiology uninteresting and difficult. I loved it.

There was a student that I had met before but didn't particularly care for. Years later we were in micro together and sat next to each other. She was the wife of my daughter, Shiranda's dad. In the micro class we became friends. The thought that I had about her was totally incorrect. In that class we realized who we were. I had thought that she was self-centered, but that was not true at all. That is why I say I am not a good judge of character. We went to the Dominican Republic together for her husband's 50th birthday. We graduated together, and she is now one of my best friends.

I believe that all you need is faith. Anything you can conceive you can achieve. Anything that you think you can do, you can. You need faith the size of a mustard seed. I heard that in church, and it is something that I have always believed. I could not give up because I had 2 kids depending on me. I wanted for my kids a better life. I wanted to be as good a mother as I could, and take the responsibility for my children. I am a living witness! If I did not have my kids I could have been a drug addict etc. but I wanted more for my life. The harder you work, the better the fruits. To whom much is given, much is required. I heard that in church too. So I am required to show grace and mercy. I am required to give back. That is just the way I am. I focus on the needs of others, but others have sometimes taken advantage of me. People might have had bad things happen to them, but that does not mean that they are bad people. I have been blessed, so I should bless others. You should do the same if you can. Remember to do unto others. So I treat people the way I want them to treat me. If I can help somebody and make it a little better for them they might not have to struggle the way I did. But if you have faith, you can make it if you try.

Sister Kathleen

KATHLEEN IS JUST three years older than I am. Growing up I was impressed with her intelligence, her quick wit, and her ability to survive. Kathleen has a strong faith in God, natural inclination to be a helper to those around her, and is willing to share vital wisdom to anyone who will listen. What follows is what she shared with me not long after her 79th birthday.

When I was 10 years old I used to wonder if there was a God that could do so many things that seemed so impossible. Was there a God who could make it rain, or snow, or make good things happen to you? When I was 13 years old I came to believe that there must be a God that made things happen; like magic. When I was saying my prayers at night it made me feel better, and made me feel happy. I was thinking that man couldn't make it rain, snow, or change the weather etc. Therefore, there had to be a God. There was something within me that told me that I should treat people nice; to do good things, period. I did find opportunities to do that. I would go to the store for older people, or help somebody without getting paid. I got a good feeling from doing such things. It made me happy, and made them happy too. When I used to live with Nanny, my grandmother on my mother's side, I used to do things for her like cooking, washing, hanging clothes on the line and all. Helping other people made me very happy. That came from home. Mommy worked all the time and I would sometimes take a bucket of water and wash the floor because she was tired. Mommy was such an understanding and compassionate person. I guess it just came up in me.

Going to church all the time, reading the Bible and learning about God just felt good!

I realized that I had to depend on God. One time I got caught in a rain storm when I was coming home from school. There was thunder and lightning all around me, but I didn't get hit. I knew the danger and I was afraid! That experience I will never forget! It made my faith stronger.

How come I got baptized in the first place, I was picking tomatoes, looked up—it seems so far-fetched. I saw it written in the sky in smoke "Believe and be baptized.". People had told me that I should be baptized and join Church etc. But I thought I needed a sign or a deeper reason. I have shared that experience only two times in the past 60 years because it seemed so far-fetched even to me. I knew that people did sky writing. I was not that deeply religious. But after that I had no doubt about God. Subsequently, about a month later I got baptized. I didn't just jump and get baptized just because people said I should.

God has used me often. When people are sick, need someone to talk to, I'm there. I have given people money in the store when they didn't have enough to buy their food. God has given me a gift of listening to people. I can sympathize with people who have problems. I talk to children who have poked fun at people with afflictions. When I was working in the Beauty Shop and children were crying I could pick them up and they would stop crying. I have dreams; clear dreams that come true. I knew about mother's death and it troubled me a lot. I can pray my pain away. I've been doing that for years.

I used to go to the Casino, and I used to smoke. God took away the desire for both of those things. God has set me free from them. I don't even think of going to the Casino now. I have had some very negative experiences. God was the only one who could help me. You know, the demons tell you you're going to get rich. They tell you to do things that you know are not right and you do it anyway.

I learned early on that God forgives you. If you tell a lie, use God's name in vain, commit adultery, back biting. God has grace. We were created by God. God is so high you can't get over Him; so low you can't get under Him, and so wide that you can't get around Him. He is the beginning and the ending. He is omnipresent, and omniscient. He can be here and somewhere with somebody else at the same time. God is someone you can believe in and trust. He is our creator. He created you and he can take you away. God really wants us to be loving people toward one another. His will is for us to be loving and forgiving. God cares for us. That is why he sent his Son to die for us. We belong to God. God doesn't owe us a thing. Healing, sight, health--. Who else could do the things he does?

When I had the fire I lost the children in the fire. I couldn't understand then. I said what kind of God would let your children burn up in a fire. "you cry and rejoice later, loss my mother. By the help of God I was able to understand those things. It has made me a better person; I can help people to understand how I have learned to understand. Lost my only son, 4 years old, a daughter age 3 and a daughter 11mos. That was very tragic and hard to understand. I said I have been a good mother, never neglected my children etc. I had moved out of the 2nd floor apt. because I didn't want my children to disturb the people under me. Only been there for two mos. Hand painted the house. That was a whole lot of years ago; 20 years ago. They would be older adults now.

My husband died Reverend. Mullins, it was a tragedy, but I had faith in God put my trust in him and I'm sure he's the one that kept me. The thing that gave me consolation was knowing that my children were in a better place.

The same thing when I found that I had to have an operation on my heart. The nurses told me that I had a lot of faith in

God because you were praying through the whole procedure. Had a block in the lower chamber. Tube from my groin to my heart. I watched the whole thing on a big screen. During the procedure I hemorrhaged, and God brought me through that. God told the doctors what to do. I have a lot to be thankful for. How I got over. There are a whole lot of things you have to be thankful for. You realize it after you get grown. Take your burdens to the Lord and leave them there. That is my hope. Trust and never doubt, and he will surly bring you out.

My Michele, said she was not a candidate for the surgery, the next day they did it and she came through fine. I know one thing; the bible says that it is a fool that says there is no God.

I know mommy had a lot of faith and trust, and prayed. I think that's where it started. Mommy had a strong faith, a lot of will power and would forgive everybody for everything. A loving and forgiving woman. I think that is why she didn't suffer before she died. When we left the hospital she had such a beautiful smile, a beautiful smile. I said mommy you look so beautiful; all you need is some lipstick. I knew she never wore lipstick. She said nothing, only smiled, and that is what I remember. Always remember Each day is not a given, it's a gift.

Psalm 139

"OH LORD, THOU hast searched me and known me. Thou knowest my down sitting and my uprising, thou understandest my thoughts from afar off. Thou compassest my path and my lying down, and thou art acquainted with all my ways. For there is not a word in my tongue, but, lo, oh Lord, thou knowest it altogether. Thou hast beset me behind and before, and laid thine hand upon me. Such knowledge is too wonderful for me, it is high, I cannot attain it. Whither shall I go from thy spirit? Or whither shall I flee from thy presence? If I ascend into heaven thou art there; if I make my bed in hell, behold, thou are there. If I take the wings of the morning, and dwell in the uppermost parts of the sea, even there shall my hand lead me, as I right hand shall hold me. If I say surely the darkness shall cover me, even the night shall be light about me. Yea; the darkness hideth not from thee, but the night shines as the day; the darkness and the light are both alike to thee. For thou hast possessed my reins, thou hast covered me in my mother's womb."

On another occasion I read in Hebrews chapter 9, verse 27. "It is appointed to man once to die, but after this the judgement" So with those words expressed in such a fiery threatening song, (you can't hide; it's no use to try) and the Holy Bible to back them up, it was enough to give the kid a good scare, if you were to think about it. I thought about a lot of things concerning God and life, and consequences of right and wrong living. Many years later, however, I began to learn a lot more about God's grace and mercy. The word mercy has been defined as what happens when God does not give us what we deserve; and grace is what happens when God gives us what we don't deserve. As I read the Bible I discovered that it is filled with stories, accounts, and illustrations of God's abundant grace and mercy.

Let's take a moment to re-examine the message in the Psalm. As we read it, we discover that God knows all about us. Now that is scary! Recently, I have been receiving a deluge of e-mail messages and advertisements from companies promising to provide a lot of sensitive personal information about anyone, for a price. They claim to have access to all existing records and files. I sincerely believe that some companies play on the urge or desire that some people have to frame or malign the character of another. There are those who wish to use such information for either personal or political advantage. It is also true that some people do not want to be known completely for fear of what may be revealed about them. It is also true that some people have such low self-esteem or such a low opinion of themselves that they cannot imagine anyone thinking well of them. One day a dejected young man I met and took to be a friend of mine said to me, "If you really knew me, you wouldn't be caught in public with me." I really didn't think it would have made a difference. I thought I knew Randolph well, but I could not be sure that what he said was not true. He was a friend that I trusted and respected.

But picture this! God speaks to each one of us individually and says, "I know you. I know all about you. I know your history. I knew you before you were born. I know your hopes, your sorrows, and your joys. I know all of your secrets. I know whom you love. I know who and what you hate. I know every move you make. I know your plans and your thoughts; all of them. I know absolutely everything about you. As a matter of fact, I know what you're thinking right now. I am omniscient. I know everything. But I still accept you. Even if everyone in the world rejects you, I will still accept you. If you want to know the truth, I really, really love you! That is why I sent my Son to die that terrible death on the cross for your sins. I am God Almighty. I am Holy, and I am your friend!"

Randolph might have been right when he said if I had known everything about him I might not have given him the time of day. But God's love is unconditional. We cannot do anything to cause God to love us any more or any less. The

Bible teaches us what true unconditional love is in First John. It says that God demonstrated to us how much he loved us by sending his son into the world to die and to conquer death so that we might have everlasting life through him.

The other passage of scripture that I mentioned earlier—Hebrews 9:27—also speaks of God's special love. The complete sentence reads "—and just as it is destined that each person dies only once, and after that, judgment comes, so also Christ died once, as a sacrifice to take away the sins of many people."

What it means is that all people die a physical death. The heart stops beating; the body stops functioning; the brain waves stop, and the person dies. But since we are spiritual beings as well as physical beings, physical death is not the end for us. There is a part of us that is not physical, but spiritual. You could say that our spirit is our main connection to God. When our physical body dies, our spiritual body continues to live. Christians believe that after we die, our spirit lives on with the Lord in Heaven forever.

The more I study the Bible the more I understand that God loves us and wants us to enjoy all of the blessings of creation, of God's presence, and of fellowship with one another. I have always found fellowship in the church. That was very important to me when I was growing up, and more than ever, it is important to me now.

When I was twelve years old, I went to live with my sister Bernice who had married a Baptist preacher, the Reverend T. B. Scott. He became the Senior Pastor of the First Baptist Church of Bel Air. It was while I was living with Bernice that I met my first girlfriend, sang my first solo, took my first piano lesson, traveled to many different churches, and learned quite a bit about the contents of the Bible. I always get a warm feeling inside when I think about the "Joel Gospel Singers" a group of teenagers who had formed a singing group. I was the pianist. We had a good time, and our parents were proud of us. The pastor had a good addition to his sermon, and visitors were always spiritually lifted.

It was also at the age of twelve that I felt an urge, and then a definite need to be baptized. In those days the water in the baptismal pool was not heated, at least it wasn't heated that day in February when I was baptized by immersion. It was an experience that I shall never forget. Baptism was very important to me, and I took it very seriously. I had decided that I wanted to "Get right with God." I wanted to be good and faithful. I must confess, however, that it wasn't long before I began to slip back into some of the ways of the world. When that sort of thing happened, some of the church members would say that we had gone down into the water with a dry devil and came up with a wet one. What they meant is that our baptism didn't mean a thing. But my baptism did mean a lot to me. It was very special.

Although I did not at the time really change my ways, I knew that I had somehow gotten closer to God. I was also aware that I had moved to a stronger religious position in the faith community. I knew that from that time on, that God would take control of my life.

Although I had not yet accepted Jesus as my savior, and really didn't understand the process, or what it really meant, my baptism was very meaningful to me. I had been down in the water and felt closer to God who had been down in the grave and had risen from the dead. I certainly had a lot to learn about the Person and work of Jesus Christ and what it meant to follow Jesus, but for me it was a good start. If I had been brought up in the Methodist church instead of the Baptist church, I would probably have been baptized as an infant. In the United Methodist church, we baptize infants, and we believe that in some mysterious way they experience God's presence at that time.

John Wesley, the founder of the Methodist church, taught that when we come before the congregation to present the child for baptism, God's grace comes before us and meets us there. He called it prevenient grace, or "grace that comes before."

Belief in God has always been a given in my family. My grandfather Solomon was a lay preacher in the African Methodist Episcopal Church. My Uncle Lueray Norris taught voice, piano, and organ for many years. He was also a church musician for all of his functioning life. My father, Mr. Clarke Andrew Green, seldom attended church because he was unhappy with most preachers, at least it seems that way to us by the way he spoke about them. Maybe it had something to do with his own life-style, for he would quickly admit that he himself was no saint. However, I do remember being taken to church at an early age by my mom and my dad together. My father also never ate a meal without first washing his face, combing his hair lightly, and bowing his head to whisper a prayer of thanksgiving; every member of my family could testify to that.

We listened every Sunday morning to religious music on radio station WASA in Havre de Grace, Maryland. Church services and church sponsored activities were practically the only regular opportunities for recreation and fellowship for us at the time. I graduated from Central Consolidated School located in Hickory, Maryland, about 3 miles north of Bel Air. After high school I moved to Baltimore where I attended Morgan State College, now Morgan State University. There were in my life other years, other experiences including military service, and other adventures not unimportant, but not included in this sketch.

But now I would like for you to meet some very important people. Their stories are true, but some of the names have been changed in order to preserve individual and family integrity.

An Ordinary Person

AT THE TIME I was interviewing Andres he was 24 years old. He was born in a small town in Mexico. Andres is one of eight children; four boys and four girls. He has two brothers who are currently living in the United States. The rest of the family is in Mexico. Andres is very close to his mother; he has always felt that way. Food and clothing were always available for him as far as he can remember. Andrés said that he could not remember ever being hungry.

"As a child I have always been healthy-mentally and physically. I have always loved to play with my friends. As a teenager growing up, I had a part-time job on Saturdays and attended school during the week. I began to earn a little money, but I got interested in partying, and my grades began to fall. I remember that one of my sisters bought shoes and books for me. As time passed and I continued to do poorly in school, not showing genuine interest in my studies, my sister stopped helping me. Pretty soon my mom gave me an ultimatum. She told me that I would have to either study or work. She made it clear that I had to become more responsible.

"Since my father was not too attached to the family, my older sister helped my mother to raise the children. I continued to live in kind of a slump for a couple of years. However, I did manage to finish school and I did get a job selling baby clothing. After spending two and a half years on that job I came to the United States. I have been in this country for three and a half years. I got here by walking through the desert. I didn't really have that many problems coming across. For example, I did not get cold or hungry. It was a blessing for me that I did not get sick, or injured. I was not bitten by any snakes or scorpions, or attacked by any wild animals. Also, I was not caught by the authorities. By the way, when I came into this country, I paid 1800 pesos, which was the equivalent of about

$2000. Now the going rate is about 3000 pesos or even double the former amount. There is actually no fixed price."

"Most Mexicans and South Americans believe in God. Most of them are Catholic. However, I am a Christian believer. I remember going to church with my mother on Christmas Eve and at the end of the year by tradition. Most children in Mexico and South America are taught to believe in God, and they actually do believe in God. There, everyone knows that there is a God and that Jesus is the Son of God. Everyone crosses himself or herself and says the Lord's Prayer before going to bed. But I had learned to believe in other images that had nothing to do with God.

"I was in the United States when I accepted Christ as my personal savior. A friend came to talk to me about it. I became interested, went to his church and made a profession of faith. The reason I went to church was that I was afraid of what was going to happen. I saw the hand of the Lord moving- things I saw with my own eyes. Wow! I began to read the Bible. In fact, I started reading the Bible almost every day. My spirit needed to be in communion with God. I had made a confession of faith; it was not by obligation; it was my own desire. It was something that I actually wanted to do. I wanted to get closer to God. In order to get closer to God, you need to pray and read the Bible. At first they told me, but later I found out for myself. Now I want more! I like to share the Word. There comes a deeper call after a while. I talk to my family and friends about God.

"I don't go to parties anymore; I get more joy out of going to church. I feel accepted by the Church and the people. Some people don't want to hear about the nature of God, the love of God, or the Bible. They look at me like I'm crazy. I know that if God is for us no one can really be against us.

"Jesus said that many people would enter the wide door, but few would enter the narrow door. For many reasons I have felt that my life and the lives of the people of the world are not in God's will, and therefore, are lost. I have seen God's hand at work in my life during the time when I was fifteen, sixteen, and seventeen. I was normal, but that part of my life was wasted; useless, without value. Other people used to tell me the same thing. But when I came here and became acquainted with Jesus, I felt a value in my life. I started to live a different way. I started a brand-new life. I feel much better now. God brought me to this country in order that I might know him. So that is the best thing that ever happened to me.

"I want to share the good news all over the world and to immerse myself in God's Spirit, in God's presence, and to share the experience with my family and the world. I want to maintain my position in Christ. Nothing can move me! I want to get nearer and nearer to Christ. I want to be used according to his purpose. I do believe God is using me in both the White Church and in the Spanish Church. I am telling the story of what God is doing in my life. I am leading prayer in Spanish worship. I do believe that God is calling me now to carry the Word in the new and intensive way; I don't know how just yet. I feel that I am being called to do a lot of things for the glory of his name. God, I feel, is giving me more challenges, perfecting His word in me."

When I asked Andres why he thought people risked their lives to get into the United States, he said that the primary motive is the economic situation in Mexico. He said you could work in Mexico, but the salary is very low. He insisted that life is expensive both here and Mexico, and it is difficult both places, although it is easier here. He continued to say that it is obviously more difficult when you have a family. One big problem according to Andres is that the families are separated. Time passes; they make money and they forget all about their families. He emphasized the fact that for him it was a blessing to come into the United States, and the reason that it was such a blessing is that because it was here that he met Jesus Christ and accepted him as his personal Lord and Savior.

An Ordinary Woman

NOEMÍ PEREZ WAS born in Puerto Rico. "I was baptized at age 15. The Pentecostal church of which my family was a part believed in baptism by immersion. My baptism took place in Humacao. It was necessary to get baptized in order to have the rights and privileges of membership. I have believed in God since childhood. I can't remember a time when I did not believe in God. I have always believed in a God of love, a God who loves to me. I grew up believing that if I was bad God would scold me and punish me. As a child I never went to the movies; that was bad. It was of the world. The church was very strict.

"My father and my mother had quite a bit of influence on my life. My father was very strong and healthy. He was also very patient. I considered my father to be a holy man. He was a peace loving man. He never offended anyone. My dad never raised his voice. I was not forced to go to church. We went because we wanted to. I really went to church because I wanted to please my father. He always saw me as a leader. Papi encouraged me to become a missionary since women were not accepted as Pastors. At first I didn't want to go to the institution to become a missionary, but I finally decided to do it.

"My husband had been a member of the same church. That was a good thing because I could not be unequally yoked with an unbeliever. My father's church was very strict. My husband retired after working for many years for the government of Puerto Rico. My middle son wanted to study in the United States. When we moved here to support him in his educational pursuits, I started to study English at a local state college, which is now a university.

"I received my call to ministry in Puerto Rico. I recall very clearly that I was sitting in church on the last bench. There was a young man playing a trumpet solo. The song he was playing was a song that means there were 100 sheep. It was a very touching hymn about the biblical parable where the man who had a hundred sheep and one went astray. It tells how the shepherd left the 99 sheep to go out into the desert and took great risks and made great sacrifices to find the lost sheep to bring it back to the fold. I felt that I was that lost sheep. This, for me, was a new experience. I had been a Christian by tradition, but I had sworn that I would never be neither a pastor nor a missionary. I also promised that I would never marry a pastor. I had been affected by the abuse of my father and my family by the church. I realized that God was calling me for something. By the time the young man finished playing, I found myself at the altar. It was clear to me that I had been writing my own life story. I was 26 years old when I had that experience.

"I had been taking care of my father who was a paraplegic. He had lost the use of both of his arms and hands. He had not been able to move his hands for months. I had been taking care of both of my parents both day and night. One day, when I took his hand he squeezed my hand very tightly. It was a sign or message to me. I promised to take my father's place, to save the souls that he had missed. My father died that day, and my mother died a week later. I did become a missionary in the Pentecostal church where I worked for a long time.

"When I came here, I went immediately to the Pentecostal church, but did not feel welcomed there. My nephew was playing the piano in the Methodist Church, so I started going there with him. Now I felt welcomed. I soon became a member of that church and later got involved in religious studies in pursuit of Pastoral ministry. I also studied at Glassboro State College at the same time. I finished Glassboro with a bachelor's degree in sociology. Later, I became an associate member of the Southern New Jersey Annual Conference of the United Methodist Church.

"My most difficult challenge in ministry came when church members, including people in leadership, rejected my ministry. Some of the problems I've faced were: racism, a wrong understanding of the Church, and an unwillingness to share and work together in ministry. Some church leaders were especially critical and seemed to claim personal ownership of the church. At times I felt unwelcome and unsupported. Leadership would not accept my vision. I lived through a very difficult struggle. I knew I had a call for ministry and to build a church. I had with me 18 people who would not give up. I knew I had a definite call to ministry. I knew that I had a certain responsibility to God and to Latino people. I knew that God was always in the picture. God has given many blessings. Having support from Christian sisters and brothers, however, gave us incentives to trust in an all-powerful, all-knowing, and compassionate God. Finding a central location for a church was also a gift from God.

"Having a spouse who is a believer and totally supportive is another special blessing from God. My husband is a very talented person who has a background in administrative matters, and, is well organized. He has a tremendous business sense. He also makes extra efforts, many sacrifices, in order to support my ministry. He has a very good command of the English language and is musically talented, as well. God has also blessed my ministry through my sons who have been faithful, supportive, and have never given us any trouble."

With joy, Noemí fought long and hard against great odds in order to realize the vision that God had given her to build a church. Besides being a woman in a male dominated world, and besides being a minority, she was an outsider. One older gentleman said one day, "Here you are an outsider unless you have been here for over twenty years. If you've been here for twenty years, then you're one of the new people." He was not speaking in jest.

In every aspect and phase of her ministry Noemí exemplified caring, conviction, the love of Christ, and great faith! Throughout the project, life for her was a tremendous struggle, but she had a vision, and she would not quit until that vision became a reality.

Pastor Noemí did build a church in the same town where her life and her ministry had met with the greatest challenges. Oasis United Methodist Church has an average Sunday morning attendance of over one hundred. The ministry reaches people in Pleasantville, New Jersey, Atlantic City, and beyond. The people who are involved in or who benefit from the ministry are Hispanic/Latinos, African Americans, and others. Everyone is welcome, and God is using the ministry to reach new people for Christ. Premarital, and other Pastoral Counseling are also available.

Two Ordinary People

MRS. LU WAS born in Shanghai, China. She has seven brothers and sisters. "My mother was a Christian. I have been influenced by my grandfather, as well. He studied medicine in a school near Beijing, and he was a successful surgeon. There was an experience that my grandfather had as a young man. It seemed to that one day, while walking down the street, he heard the sound of a group of Christians singing. He was touched by them, and their loving attitude toward one another. Getting to know some of them was touched by their example. He became a very good Christian, and later began to preach the Gospel. This was during the Boxer Rebellion.

The Boxer Rebellion, Boxer Uprising or Yihequan Movement was a violent anti-foreign and anti-Christian uprising which took place in China towards the end of the Qing dynasty between 1899 and 1901. It was initiated by the Militia United in Righteousness (*Yihetuan*), known in English as the "Boxers", and was motivated by proto-nationalist sentiments and opposition to imperialist expansion and associated Christian missionary activity. An Eight-Nation Alliance invaded China to defeat the Boxers and took retribution.[5]

"Fortunately, my grandfather was able to escape. My mother was a member of the Christian Missionary Alliance Church. She was educated through the city school system. My mother really loved the Lord and was always involved in many aspects of the Church. She was a very strict parent who made sure that all of the children attended Sunday school. The children were not allowed to follow worldly trends. We never experienced any of the secular night life that would have normally been available to us. My father was a Christian also,

---

[5] Information on the Boxer Rebellion from Wikipedia

but not as dedicated as my mom. He became a Christian later in life. I was raised in a Christian environment. All of my teachers were Christians.

When I was 17, I remember going with my mother to a small church meeting. The thing that impressed me was that people really loved the Lord, and they were so good to one another. The preacher preached and I was touched. I had been raised in a Christian family, but the truth is that I had felt weak. At that time, I made a personal commitment to Jesus Christ, accepting him as my Lord and Savior. From that time on I have done all that I could do to please God, such as reading the Bible, praying, and emphasizing the personal relationship with Christ.

Before the Communists came, it was not that difficult to be a Christian. But you have to be strong. My mother didn't allow any dancing and no movies. When your schoolmates are involved in secular activities, you are obviously very different. You have to resist the peer pressure. But I wanted to be like that! I would always pray before meals every day. I had been raised in a strict Christian environment, but from the age of 17, I have loved the Lord for myself.

"The Communists first occupied the northern and western parts of China, so we had heard a lot about them. During the first few years of their occupation the Communists did not do much to bother the Christians, but then later they wanted to control everything. In our church the Christians were very serious, and there were a lot of educated members. The young people chose to follow

Christ rather than the government. That made the government very angry.

"The first thing the Communists did was to take over the property of the rich and accuse them of exploiting the people. They accused the capitalists of being evil. Now capitalism is encouraged. Former Communist leaders now become very rich and much richer than formal capitalists. My grandfather, having been a successful surgeon, was accused of being a capitalist since he was a successful businessman. Anyone who had money or property was regarded as evil. Grandfather, therefore, became a target and left and went to Hong Kong. In 1960 he came to America, leaving all of his property in China. He never regretted coming to the United States. He came with four children. He was very devoted to the Lord. He worked and lived a simple life.

"During the first five years of communism Christian life was normal. After five or six years passed, the Communists started a political campaign against the church. It was called the Self-Government movement. Christianity was from the West. The government accused the Chinese Christians of being influenced by the West, and told them that they had to be independent from the West. They ordered them to obey the government and not the church leaders from the West. They were admonished to run their own church. Those who would not follow the admonition of the government were called counter-revolutionaries. Many young Christians were arrested and sent to labor camps. A strong Christian leader who wanted to follow the Bible and not the government was called counter-revolutionary.

In 1956 all of the important church leaders who were not in the self-government movement were arrested and put in jail. Churches were allowed to remain open, but the government had to approve all sermons. Leaders were not allowed to preach from the book of Genesis or from the book of Revelation because those books teach of God creating the world and Christ's return in power and glory. Many young Christians were arrested and sent to labor camps. A strong Christian leader who wanted to follow the Bible and not the government was called the counter-revolutionary. Christians paid a high price to follow Jesus. Very prominent young Christians with promising futures were sent to labor camp for 20 years.

Today people have more freedom in China, but still, if you are an influential leader, the government will take notice of you. You can be a Christian by yourself, but if you have a church in your own home, the government will take notice of you. There are many Christians in Har Nan Province and San Douy province where entire villages have come to the Lord.

The government permits just a few churches where there are five or six meetings each Sunday.

Mrs. Lu studied in China; her mother was a piano teacher. Mrs. Lu, herself, taught piano at the Shanghai Conservatory, once known as the best in China. I found Mrs. Lu to be a very strong Christian woman. It was a delight to be in her home and to share with her a cup of Chinese tea which she prepared for me during an interview with her. While she was reluctant to talk much about her own Christian witness, she spoke to me several times about a man by the name of Watchman Nee. She said that he was the greatest influence in bringing Christianity to China in modern times.

Watchman Nee, whose Chinese name was Nee Shu-tau, was born in 1903 in Foochow, China. His parents were second generation Christians. He had been consecrated to the Lord before he was born. Because he was the third child preceded by two sisters, and because he had an aunt who had six daughters in succession, there was some displeasure in the family when his mother had two girls. But his mother prayed to the Lord, saying, and "If I have a boy, I will present him to you." The Lord heard her prayer and he was born.

Before the moment of his salvation Nee She-tsu did not conduct himself well as a student. He had been described as ill-behaved." He was always able to meet every academic challenge, however. His exceptional intelligence was known to his peers as well as to his teachers. In 1920, at the age of 17, Nee became saved... For him it was a dynamic experience! In his own words, "I was saved in 1920 at the age of 17. Before being saved I experienced some mental conflict concerning whether or not to accept the Lord Jesus as my savior and whether or not to become a devoted servant. For most people the problem at the time of salvation is how to be delivered from sin. But for me, being saved from sin and my life career were linked together. If I were to accept the Lord Jesus as my savior, I would simultaneously accept him as my Lord. He would deliver me not only from sin, but also from the world. At that time, I was afraid of being saved, for I knew that once I was saved, I must serve the Lord. Of necessity, therefore, my salvation would be a duel salvation. It was impossible for me to set aside the Lord's calling in order to desire only salvation. I had to choose either to believe in the Lord and have a duel salvation or forfeit both. For me to accept the Lord would mean that both events would take place simultaneously."

Watchman Nee did make that final decision. "On the evening of April 29th, 1920, I was alone in my room. I had no peace of mind. Whether I sat or reclined, I could find no rest; coming from within was the problem of whether or not I should believe in the Lord. My first inclination was not to believe in the Lord Jesus and not to become a Christian. However, that made me inwardly uneasy. There was a real struggle within me. Then I knelt down to pray. At first I had no words with which to pray. But eventually many scenes came before me, and I realized that I was a sinner. I have never had such an experience in my life before that time. I saw myself as a sinner and I also saw the Savior. I saw the filthiness of sin and I also saw the efficacy of the Lord's precious blood cleansing me and making me white as snow. I saw the Lord's hands nailed to the cross, and at the same time I saw him stretching forth his arms to welcome me, saying I am here waiting to receive you.' Overwhelmed by such a love, I could not possibly reject it, and I decided to accept him as my Savior. Previously I had laughed at those who believed in the Lord, but that evening I could not laugh. Instead, I wept and confessed my sins, seeking the Lord's forgiveness. After making my confession, the burden of my sins was discharged, and I felt buoyant and full of inward joy and peace. This was the first time in my life that I knew I was a sinner. I prayed for the first time, and had my first experience of joy and peace. There might have been some joy and peace before, but the joy after my salvation was very real! Alone in my room I saw the light and lost all consciousness of my surroundings. I said to the Lord, "'Lord, you have really been gracious to me."

He knew that he had been raised up by the Lord to carry out a commission. Therefore, he adopted an English name, Watchman, because he felt that he had been raised up to sound a warning call on God's behalf.

Watchman Nee was a "native preacher." He did not attend any seminaries or Bible schools. However, he did acquire a wealth of knowledge about God's purpose in the world, Jesus Christ, the Holy Spirit, and the church. He learned all he knew by studying the Bible and by reading Christian literature. Watchman studied diligently using 20 different methods. He spent one third of his income on personal necessities, one third on charity, and one third on what he called spiritual books. Those spiritual books were 3000 of the best Christian books available. This included all of the classical Christian writers who had been published since the first century. Blessed by a phenomenal ability to select, understand, and memorize important material, Watchman obtained a sound knowledge of church history and became a prolific Christian writer himself. Early in his Christian life he had been the beneficiary of much spiritual guidance from Margaret Barber, a former Anglican missionary. Through Miss Barber, Watchman had been able to acquire many of the Christian books that he had found so helpful in his spiritual journey.

Watchman Nee received a divine revelation from the Lord assuring him of a twofold burden and commission. First, he was to be a unique witness for the crucified and risen Christ, and secondly he was to establish local churches. In faithfulness to his first burden, he produced a number of spoken and written messages on the "subjective aspect of the Lord's crucifixion and resurrection" and on "The principles of life, or the supremacy of Christ, and on God's eternal purpose."

Watchman used eight different ways to carry out the ministry that he felt God had called him to: preaching the gospel, traveling in revivals, contacting people, teaching the Bible, corresponding with people, holding conferences, holding training sessions, and producing Christian literature. Through his life and ministry approximately 400 local churches were established in China. Churches were also raised up in the Philippines and Singapore, Malaysia, Thailand, and Indonesia. In all, over 2300 churches have been established throughout the world due to the ministry of Watchman Nee and Witness Lee.

In his personal testimony recorded on October the 20th, 1936 he described his second commission: Watchman Nee said, " What the Lord revealed to me was extremely clear;" Before long he would raise up local churches in various parts of china. He said "Whenever I closed my eyes, the vision of the birth of local churches appeared---- when the Lord called me to serve him, the primary objective was not to hold revival meetings, help the people to hear more scriptural doctrines, or for me to become a great evangelist. The Lord revealed to me that he desired to build up local churches in various places to manifest himself and to bear testimony of unity on the ground of the local churches. In this way, each saint is able to function in the church and live the church life. What God wants is not individuals trying to be victorious or spiritual; he wants a corporate victorious church presented to himself.

Between 1940 and 1960 the local church in China experienced many difficulties. Based on the idea of oneness among believers, Watchman believed in one church for one city or town. He believed that the local church was won by Christ on Earth, and that geographic boundaries were the only legitimate reason to have different churches.[6]

Living Stream Ministry, a nonprofit corporation based in Anaheim, California is affiliated with the Local Church movement. It was founded in 1968, and is a good source for information about Watchman Nee, his life, witness and publications. I am very grateful for the resources they have provided which enabled me to include this very spiritual and very influential Christian in this book.

(Patterson, George N. Christianity in Communist China Waco TX World Books, 1969, pages 78-80[6]

An Ordinary Woman from Philadelphia

JACQUELYN HUGGINS WAS born on October the 22nd, 1949. She was two years old when her parents divorced. Her father wanted the children to be Catholic. Jacqueline and her siblings were moved into a foster care situation. This move was against her mother's wishes. "It was not a happy place-the living conditions were good, but the treatment was bad. We knew that our foster parents did not love us. We went to Mass every Sunday. I thought that was what religious people were like. They were mean and they went to church."

"At the same time I knew that God has a purpose for me in life. At first I thought he wanted me to become a nun. I had a mental picture of myself sitting at Jesus' feet being taught alone at the age of eight and even later that picture was always in my mind. I believed that God has a purpose on earth for me to help people plan their lives. I thought it might be through astrology. In my early 20s I thought there was no God at all. I went through a time of seeking, searching, and the general quest. I knew my work had to do with religion. I knew I was supposed to help people, but I figured it need not be true religion since religion had not helped the people I had been with. At the age of 10 my personality was already formed. Having been negatively influenced by my religious experience with my foster parents, I wanted to help people to find out where they were and what they believed. Some people I knew were involved in alternative spiritual sources, including Buddhism. My brother was involved in Buddhism. I was not interested in typical organized religion. I learned chanting, etc. in order to help people understand their thinking. My brother was going with a witch, so I learned about that, too. I also learned about what the Satanic Church did. Looking back now, and grounded by God's Holy Spirit, I knew within myself that those ways were not right. I knew that Ouija boards, for example, were counterfeit and could be 99% accurate. I remember reading in the Bible that Prophets were stoned if they were not 100% accurate.

In my mind I thought, 'When I grow up I'm going to turn people against God and the Bible.' I had been told that it was a sin to read the Bible because if you read it you would risk going to hell, and if you get a wrong interpretation, you may turn away from the Catholic Church. At that time in my life I was experiencing great fear and great disappointment."

"I still wanted to help people. I planned to target people who believed they were Christians. If they were not Christians, I would offer astrology to help them. If they were Christians, I would ask questions. If they did not know the answers, I would challenge them."

My sister became a Christian believer when she was 18. She started talking about Jesus all the time, and that turned us all off. I was invited to go to a Bible study. After saying no, I decided to go. I said 'will you let me talk?' I wanted to convince them with my ideas. I never went to that Bible study. That night God got my attention. My cat got real sick. I thought they had given it the wrong medicine. I went home totally devastated, while my cat was in the hospital dying. It was while I was at home crying about my cat that God spoke to me.

What are you planning to do? Those people are happy in what they believe. What have they done to you? I wonder to myself what if there really is a God; what if he is paying me back? But the plots seemed not to be coming from me! If there is a God, I am in trouble, because I've been telling people there is no God! Then I said, 'God, if you really exist, would you prove it to me?' "

"God did show me that he existed on three occasions. The first occasion is when I was working in a record store. There was a robbery and the manager was shot and died in my arms. I promised God I would follow him; but then, I turned to alcohol, marijuana etc., but they were no answer. Astrology was the only thing I liked, and it worked only 99% of the time. I could shock people with what I knew about them! I could hear God saying to me, ' your life is not so great, you're trying to help others, but you have never tried me.' I knew that if I turned to him I would never turn back. Should I or shouldn't I? That is when God showed me those three occasions. The second occasion was when I was pregnant and the baby was due. I was very sick and having a lot of problems; I thought I was going to die. I spoke to God then, and said, 'if you exist God, help me. And at that instant I got a pain and the baby was born that night."

I had also gotten engaged but I did not marry. I discovered that God had plans for both of us. When God does things he does them decently, and in order. When we got saved, we became like brother and sister.

I said, "God what do you want me to do?" God told me that I should get a Bible and look up the word repentance. I found it in Romans, chapter 2 verse four. In the New Living translation of the Bible it reads: "Don't you realize how kind, tolerant, and patient God is with you? Or don't you care? Can't you see how kind he has been in giving you time to turn from your sin?" In his kindness,

God sometimes exercises extra grace by withholding his judgment against us, giving us the time to turn from sin. Sometimes we mistake God's patience for approval of the wrong way we are living. It is difficult for us to evaluate ourselves, and it is even more difficult to come to God and let him tell us where we need to change. As Christians we must ask God to point out our sins, in order that he might heal us. I kept reading that verse over and over. The more I read the stronger I thought, 'If I say I'm sorry, will God forgive me? Wow! Wouldn't that be something! I'm sorry; I didn't know that was repentance! I instantly knew that I was forgiven! I felt so free! I wanted to go back to business as usual. But I knew I could no longer do astrology. I asked my sister Ashley about astrology. She said that astrology worked through the power of the devil. I burned all of my books. I could not go back to business as usual. I had to tell all of my friends. I started to think of new ways to talk to people. I would ask them if they were a Christian. That would start a conversation. I never got tired of talking about Jesus."

An advertisement for Wycliffe Bible Translators caught Jacqueline's attention. Since she had an interest in linguistics and foreign languages, and since she had come to the conclusion that God communicates with us through his written word, Jacqueline thought that this would be a place where God could use her. After a time of procrastination, she submitted the application, went through a period of intensive training, and was sent to the Philippines to work as a Bible Translator. She has been with Wycliffe since 1984. God called Jacqueline to live and work among the Kagayanan people. Since she has been on the island, children have been born, grown up, married, and have had children of their own.

In April of 2008, Wycliffe Bible Translators held a dedication service to celebrate the completion of the New Testament for the Kagayanan people in the Philippines. Jackie, as she is known by her close friends and family, was the first African-American woman to complete a New Testament translation in a formerly unwritten language. Jacqueline, who likes to give all the credit to God and others would quickly admit that the translation was a team effort. Jacqueline, however, was the team leader.

I first interviewed Jackie on the same day of the dedication. As an African-American pastor, I had been invited by the Wycliffe organization to witness that historic occasion. It was my first trip to the Philippines. I found the people there to be very warm, kind, mild-mannered, very polite and patient. I also found many Christians there. We were all given a copy of the New Testament translation *PULONG TA DYOS, GENESIS DAW BAG-O NA* KASUGTANAN. It is the New Testament, and the Book of Genesis.

Jacqueline wants everyone to know that, "God has a plan for your life. He has a plan for every individual in the world. If you will strive to carry out God's plan for you, you will be totally fulfilled, and you will be a blessing to the world!"

Jacqueline has continued to work and study. She began a study program in June 2011. She has completed work on a PhD in Anthropology. The title of her dissertation is; **THE ETHNOGRAPHY OF READING AMONG THE KAGAYANEN OF PALAWAU: A MIRO-STUDY OF THE NEGLECTED DIMENSION OF READING COMPREHENSION.** She graduated on June 26, 2016.

Two More Ordinary People

TWO VERY ORDINARY people who have been used greatly by God are Henry and Ella Appenzeller. Most of the information included here about these two Godly people has been extracted from a paper that had been thoroughly researched by the Reverend Kenneth E. Kroehler, Senior Pastor of the First United Methodist Church in downtown Lancaster, Pennsylvania. Reverend Kroehler said, "The story of these pioneering missionaries had caught my attention because of their membership and marriage in the First United Methodist Church at Lancaster. Because of the traditions of this congregation they have kept alive the memory of Henry and Ella, and even more so, because of the frequent visitors each year from Korea who want to see The Appenzeller Church. My interest has been at first piqued, then awed by the lasting contribution of these extraordinarily ordinary people to the faith, culture, and politics of Korea."

Reverend Gerhard Appenzeller was a Methodist who was one of the missionaries instrumental in introducing Protestant Christianity into Korea. He was born in February of 1858 in Souderton, Pennsylvania. His mother was from a Swiss Mennonite family, and his father was a Pennsylvania Dutchman of the fourth generation. Henry's mother, who was largely responsible for his religious formation, used to sit him down with his two brothers on Sunday afternoons and read to them from the German Bible. It was convenient for her to teach them in German since she spoke very little English. Henry spoke "Pennsylvania German" until he was twelve. He did learn German very well, and used it all of his life, even communicating with Germans in Korea.

Henry memorized the Heidelberg Catechism, which emphasized personal faith. When he learned the Catechism, he learned the Ten Commandments, the Apostles' Creed, the

Lord's Prayer, and an intellectual type of piety. Since Mr. Appenzeller did not accept infant baptism, Henry and his brothers were baptized after making their own affirmation of faith.

At the age of 18 during the time that he was preparing for college at the West Chester Normal School, Henry experienced a significant religious transformation. The local Presbyterian Church was having special services with a guest evangelist. On October 6, 1876 Henry had a deep personal experience and celebrated that date each year as his spiritual birthday. He then organized a prayer group that provided impetus for the YMCA in West Chester.

At his father's prompting, he attended Franklin and Marshall College, which was a school that was deeply rooted in the reformed church. While at college, he fell in with a bunch of Methodists and began visiting area churches. Henry had learned discipline and kept a strict diary. According to his diary, during a time of spiritual restlessness, he was attracted to the class meetings at First Episcopal Church. On April 16, 1879, his diary reflects that he was studying the minutes of the Philadelphia conference, and was impressed, to the point that on the following Sunday, he joined First Church. He recorded: "This step is taken only after prayer and meditation for some time. Since my conversion on October 1, 1876, I have been among the Methodists most of my time and feel more at home than I did in the reformed church, and I feel it to be my duty to join the M. E. Church, and what I did today I did with an eye single to the glory of God." The very next Sunday, he joined First Church. After he joined First Church, Henry became an assistant Pastor while attending college. He served what has now become Broad Street Methodist. Henry first recognized his call to foreign missions when he heard a sermon on missions and gave $2.50 to the cause. The following week he recorded in his diary that the ambition of his life was to spend it entirely in the service of the Lord.

It was also during his college years that Henry met Ella Dodge, a devout Christian from New York. She was a descendant of William Dodge, who had come from Chester,

England to settle in New England in 1629. Ella fell in love with Henry, joined First Church, and agreed to join him in a common call to serve Christ in foreign missions.

After graduating from Franklin and Marshall College in Lancaster, Pennsylvania in 1882, he entered Drew Theological Seminary in Madison, New Jersey. At Drew there was a lot of excitement about the fast growing missionary movement of the 19th century. Henry applied to the Board of Foreign Missions of the M.E. Church for service in Japan. There were no openings in Japan, but there were possibilities for Korea, a nation that had just signed a treaty with the U.S. The Board decided to send him and his bride, Ella, to Korea, along with a previously elected missionary Doctor William Scranton. After being ordained to the Ministry the Reverend Appenzeller was appointed as a missionary to Korea in 1885.

It was on the day after his ordination that Henry and Ella boarded the Good Ship Arabic along with Dr. Scranton, his wife and his mother. Twenty-three days of sailing took them across the pacific to Yokohama, Japan.

Arriving in Korea in April, 1885, Appenzeller established a Methodist church in Korea and traveled about the country preaching the gospel of Jesus Christ He established the first modern western type school in Korea, which was the predecessor of today's Pai Chai University. Mrs. Appenzeller and Mrs. Scranton established Ewha Hakdang School for girls in 1886, with one student. It is now Ewha Women's University, the largest women's university in the world, having 21,000 students in 14 colleges and 13 graduate schools. At last count the school had produced 140,000 graduates. The school played a tremendous role in elevating the status of women in Korea. He also worked in concert with other missionaries translating the Bible into the Korean language.

Reverend Henry Appenzeller and his wife Ella left an indelible mark on the land of Korea, and on the Methodist church. While in Korea they raised four children, instilling in them a love for global mission, and for the country. Their daughter Alice Rebecca, born on November 5, 1885 was the first Caucasian born in Korea. By the time she went to be with the Lord, Rebecca had been the longest-lived native Caucasian in that country.

In her lifetime Rebecca had many successful accomplishments. After being tutored by her mother until 1900 she came to Lancaster and graduated from the Shippen School in 1905. The Shippen `School is now the Lancaster Country Day School. She earned a B.A. from Wellesley College in Massachusetts in 1909, a Master of Arts from Columbia University, and engaged in further studies at Columbia and Harvard Universities. Alice also taught at the Shippen School, was commissioned as a Missionary of the Women's Foreign Missionary Society of the Methodist Church and assigned to EWHA University. There she served as Vice President, and later as President, for 17 years.

Alice was a woman who had a very strong, positive influence on the people of Korea who loved her very much. Her death marked a time of genuine national mourning. More than a hundred organizations and institutions representing educational, religious, social and cultural interests appointed delegates to a committee to plan and carry out the funeral services in the Chung Dong Church. That was the church that her father had organized, where she had been baptized as the first white child born in Korea, and where she was ordained. Two of the dignitaries who spoke at her funeral were the President of Korea and the American Ambassador.

From the West Gate of Seoul, which is the capital and largest city of South Korea, the cemetery was about two miles. The people gathered early in the morning to clean up the streets and fill in the holes in the broken road. The women and girls carried water from distant wells, either on their heads or on their backs. They kept watering that stretch of road until the procession had ended.

I have been informed by Pastor Kroehler that each year many Koreans come to this land to visit the church where the Appenzellers had their spiritual beginning, which was so vital to the beginnings of protestant Christianity in Korea.

Henry and Ella Appenzeller were two very ordinary

people with humble beginnings. God used them mightily as they stepped out on faith to help take Christ to Korea, and to help elevate the people to a higher level of education, and a better quality of life.

SILA

I MET SILA La Rosa at Stevens Emmanuel United Methodist Church located in the Allison Hill section of Harrisburg, Pa. I was appointed to serve there as an Interim Pastor.

Sila is a gifted and powerful preacher who is a hard worker, and takes the work of Christian Ministry very seriously. She has experienced first-hand what it means to struggle against great odds both in her native country, and in her new home that she loves; the United States of America, what it means to struggle for survival. As a black woman growing up in Communist Cuba she faced particular challenges, and, as a black female immigrant living in North America she faces a different set of challenges.

"When I was born in Cuba the political situation was bad. Racism was a social and economic reality. There were white societies and black societies. There were sports centers for blacks, and sports centers for whites.

White people owned most of the businesses, and were involved in politics. They had connections with the United States, and they were the ones who had money.

My family was poor. My father worked as a construction helper. He drank a lot. We did not have access to medical services. I had a little brother who died of diphtheria because of lack of medical help. His throat closed. The Priest came. We took him to the hospital, but he did not survive.

We had been all living in one room, but we could not stay there because of the sickness so we had to move. We went to live with my maternal grandmother where we stayed for 3 months in the country. When we returned we went to live on the property of my paternal grandfather. He had a good position.

I had a good relationship with my father. He showed me love, and I learned to love from him. I was his favorite.

I had friends who were taking classes in the Catholic school. I liked that, but we had to work. Mother took in wash, and we had to help her.

I went to the Catholic Church and said I wanted to be baptized. I took classes, and was baptized. My parents didn't know anything about it. The Revolution was going on and Castro felt that it was not good to be in Church.

My father worked under the control of The Communist Party. He used to go to the mountains to look for people who were against the Revolution. I remember that he spent months in the mountains.

Early on I had decided that I wanted to study. When I was in primary school a cousin of my father was one of my teachers. She encouraged me. I wanted to study, but we had to work in the country first. At first my mother didn't want me to go but later she agreed.

I had to work in construction during the first year. They gave classes under trees. We slept on hammocks. We were living in an area that was quite a distance away. We had to work for 9 months before we could go home. During that period the parents could visit 3 times, but my parents never visited me because my mother was asthmatic.

Then we were moved to the center of the island to a place that was reserved for tuberculosis care. We stayed there for 2 years, with a vacation after 9 months. The students had to work there also. I did construction work helping to build a school. Then we were moved to the capitol.

There we lived in a beach house and they provided us with a maid. We were given individual instruction during the day, and we taught in the school in the evening. We were under a strict disciplinary system like the Russians.

During my last year of study, they sent me to a province far away from home. I lived with a family there. In those situations, the students worked with the families in every aspect. The government called it socialization.

After that we went to the Capitol and were graduated. At that time, we received 123 Cuban pesos, which was equal to $5.00. That was our salary which we received once a month. During that time, you could buy a lot with 123 pesos.

I started to work in a school, and started to specialize. I had compassion for children with disabilities, but I could not continue to work with them so I decided to major in regular primary education.

I was promoted, and became Director of the school. We had children in classes from kindergarten to grade 7. The children were given their breakfast. In school they worked in agriculture growing many fruits and vegetables; melons, cauliflower etc. Some of the melons were for the school, and other fruits and vegetables were exported.

I continued working there for five years, and was then sent to another school as a teacher. At the same time, I started University studies. I worked every day and took classes on Saturdays twice a month for four years. For the last two years I was allowed to concentrate on my studies without working. When I finished I was awarded a master's degree in Primary Education. I had studied General Education so I was qualified to teach all classes in the school system.

I went to Germany to study math because we used the German mathematic system in Cuba. I lived in Germany for a little more than a month. I returned and taught other teachers in Cuba.

When I finished earning my Master's degree I got married, and continued working. I became a member of the Communist Youth. My family's economic condition was improving. My brother had studied, and he was in a better financial situation. A lot of people had left Cuba and come to the United States. Castro took their houses and put a lot of people in them. Our family ended up with a large house. I had gotten married and had 2 children who were in day care. My sister had gotten married. Her husband was a mechanic, and had a good job.

My husband was visited by some Cuban Americans, and he decided that he wanted to come to the USA to get away from the political problems in Cuba. His father was also in politics. He came here, and I stayed in Cuba and kept working.

My time was spent working and taking care of my two sons who were then 2 and six years old. My husband lived in the U.S. for 15 years. During that time, I was studying, working, and taking care of the boys. Although he was working in the U.S. he could not help me because he was earning very little money.

We communicated regularly, but secretly. If the government found out that I was working in Education and communicating in any way with someone in the United States I would have lost my job. I would have been accused and found guilty of not supporting the Revolution.

After living here for 13 years my husband became a U.S. citizen. Then he was able to help me to get here. They took my job away because I submitted an application to come to the U.S. under an American Government Family Unification plan. Priority was given to family members under that program.

We got no help from the Cuban government. They took an inventory of our possessions and removed everything from our homes. We were not permitted to bring anything here with us. I brought my school documents hidden because they were not permitted either.

When I first came I didn't know anyone here. The government didn't let me bring my youngest son. I left him with my husband's mother. The law stated that children had to be 16 years old before they could travel. My older son was 21. I had brought him with me. We all came here legally.

It was difficult for us. I worked in a factory with my oldest son. We both had two full-time jobs in a factory. We had to do it to take care of my baby boy in Cuba, and to help the family there. We both worked on two jobs, full-time for one year in order to get my younger son out of Cuba and to get him here.

He was 17 years old when he got here. All together I worked for 3 years with my older son in the factory. Then I started looking for a job working with children because that was my profession. At first I found a Day Care in Harrisburg, but that job did not require my level of skills and training. But there was a Christian organization that met in a Catholic church that helped new immigrants. They had heard about me and about my educational background and told me where I could find work that suited my preparation. I did find a job opportunity in a private school, Kinder Care, where I have been working ever since.

My husband had come to the U.S. many years before me and got involved with other women with whom he had other children; five children in all. When I arrived here I got a divorce within 3 months. At that time, I didn't know my rights, and I didn't know anything about the laws. Not knowing where to get help I felt very much alone.

I just kept working and doing the best that I could. The three of us were living in a 2 room apartment. We lived that way for two years, then my oldest son got married and moved out, but my youngest son kept living with me.

I received a lot of help from this country. First I was permitted to work and bring my children here to a better quality of health and life in general. It also opened for me the door to a religious life. I was permitted and encouraged to go to church and to participate in religious activities.

The church here has been my refuge. It was in the church that I found a family, especially in the United Methodist Church in Harrisburg, Pa. In the church I found a different life. My whole life was arranged and settled in the church. There I was no longer lonely, but I found joy. The church showed me a different life. It took care of us in times of sickness and grief, and supplied our needs in many ways. My life was drastically changed when I met Christ, but I met Christ within the church.

In Cuba I had no knowledge of Christ. I knew that there was a god, but I did not know him. God was unknown to me. In Cuba there were many cultures; people worshipped many gods; somewhat like the ancient Greeks. There was no knowledge of salvation. The population knew nothing about the greatness, or the power, or the love of God.

When I arrived here I went and listened to the Word of God. I began to read the Bible. The Lord kept leading me and teaching me and showing me.

Back in Cuba I went secretly to a Baptist church to see a film about the Life of Christ. I felt within myself the humility of offering the other cheek. That is what touched me. It was as if the Lord was speaking to me. I didn't know what it meant, but I taught my sons, "If they hit you on one cheek turn the other." I never forgot that scene.

The major turning point in my Christian life was when I went to the Walk to Emmaus. The walk to Emmaus is a 3-day experience open to all denominations designed to strengthen the faith of Christians and to encourage Discipleship in families. During my Walk to Emmaus the Lord entered my heart. I experience the reality of the living Christ in me. In that experience the Lord changed me completely. For me it was a divine transformation! Now I belong to Christ and Christ belongs to me!

If you are confused about God my advice to you is to listen to people who know Christ, observe the way they live, and be open to the movement of the Spirit of God in your life. Try to understand that Christ died for our sins. That is the key. When you know the Lord it a new birth. I know because I have received him. The hope that I have is that one day I will see my Lord in all of his glory, and to enjoy the promises I have in the Bible. I have faith that I will see my Savior face to face.

JR

"I WAS BORN in College Point; New York City near La Guardia Airport. My father was Lead Bombardier on B17s in the 2nd World War. He was always a Godly man; stopped and helped people. He never cursed. His parents wanted him to be a priest. His sister became a Nun. There were only two of them. All of the members of the family were devout Catholics; but biblically literate.

I always had an idea about God in my life. It was the way my family lived. They instilled that faith in me. My grandmother sat on the Blessed Mary side. In the church there were two sides. The center isle was where you saw Jesus on the cross. The left side was the Mary side, and the right side was the Joseph side. So grandmother always sat on the Mary side, and grandfather always sat in the choir. He was the lead tenor. From the early 50s to the late 60s he ran the choir. If that had been a Synagogue, he would have been the Cantor. I loved to sit in the choir and sing with grandfather. I had the special privilege of singing there because of grandfather Phillip Rogers. I had two aunts who were Dominican Nuns. The family thought I would become a priest. I was an altar boy until I was 16. I loved the work.

Between the ages of 18 and 20 I only went to church on special occasions.

I was always interested in fire-fighting, ambulance, and medical First-responder work. I always wanted to be a fireman. My toys consisted of Fire trucks, Fire boats, ambulances, medical kits. The Fire department started a Junior Fireman's club. I always wanted to be either a Fireman, Medical Doctor or a Priest. We met during school nights. When I was 18, drills were always held on Sunday morning. Therefore, I fell away from regular church attendance. Then I started to get involved in special events in the Fire Department; started to smoke, etc. I knew the way, but I was not following it. A middle-aged cop told me that he had left the church, gotten married, and had children, and then came back. Speaking to a group of boys and girls in a catechism class he said that most of us would do the same thing.

In an EMT training class I met Debbie. Her father and grandfather were ex chiefs of a nearby fire company. I knew her parents but I didn't know that they were her parents. Debbie worked as a Dispatcher; receiving and transmitting all emergencies in Ronkonkoma township. I worked at Centereach Fire Company. In 1981 we had an opportunity to work together during an emergency situation. When the emergency was under control I called her again and invited her to go to a wedding with me. We were working on the 12-8 shift. When she asked when the wedding was taking place I told her, "today at 1:00pm". We were just getting off at 8:00am. The rest is history.

There were some concerns about family and church backgrounds. For generations my family had been Catholic, and her family had been United Methodist. But everything worked out. We got married in a Lutheran church. Debbie was a good Christian woman, and she led me back to church. I started going back when we were dating. I enjoyed the small church atmosphere and the coffee hour every Sunday. There I met a lot of good Christian people. In the Catholic Church we were not encouraged to go to any other churches for worship.

The Catholic Church that I had attended had a membership of close to 2,000. We had six different services. Debbie's church had about 50 people, and service was at 10:00am. Everybody knew everybody.

Over the years I have seen God's hand at work through being able to help suffering people. I had a bad accident in November of 1989. It was an ambulance accident, and I broke three ribs. I was attending a patient in the ambulance when the accident happened. I think God was slowing me down.

In 1990 Debbie became pregnant with our first son. I stopped smoking, cut down on consumption of alcohol. This was God's way of slowing me down. For my entire life I knew that God and Jesus were there and looking after me. I was in a bad accident in the winter of 1988. My car struck ice, spun, and crashed into a pole. The next thing I knew I was standing on the sidewalk. There was a man hitting me, trying to get me to respond, to bring me out of my daze, or whatever it was. I said, "Why are you hitting me?" He said, "Look at your car." The entire driver's part of the car was missing. Then he was gone.

When the cops got there they were surprised that I was even alive. I said, "That black fellow helped me." The cop said, "There's nobody here." Debbie said, "That was your angel." That was a very humbling experience. I often think back to that experience and I ask why did I survive? God had another plan for me. You can never figure out God's intentions.

To me the most amazing scripture is John 3; 16; God's forgiveness for my sins. At Calvary Baptist Church the Pastor taught me and Debbie about Baptism and about being born again. He solidified what I always knew. God is God! Jesus is Jesus! There is no second guessing. We can do all things through Christ. There is no other way. God gives us 2nd and 3rd chances. He is amazing! I had had some confusion about being born again; but if you have it, it is not going to go away from you!

On September 11th, 2001 I was on duty as a Fireman with the New York City Fire Department, engine #294. I was on a 24-hour shift. The morning of the attacks on the United States

I was on House Watch watching the news when the 1st plane hit the North Tower. Somebody is always on watch at the Fire house. That person responds to all emergencies, but does not stay there. At my Fire house there were 11 of us on duty to respond to fires. We had an engine and ladder truck; a tiller. A tiller truck is also known as a hook and ladder truck. It has two drivers with separate steering wheels for the front and rear wheel. The man in the back is called the tiller driver. It was also the time for change of tours, so there were about 20 firemen present at the time.

I notified all members in quarters that the World Trade Center North Tower was on fire. All members immediately started preparing for a response. On TV I saw a second plane hit the hit the North Tower. We all knew that it was a terrorist attack. At that point everyone started calling their houses to let their families know that we were about to be called. As soon as I got off the phone with Debbie, Engine 294, my company was ordered to respond. I drove Engine 294 and was praying the whole time. I can't tell you everything that was going through my head at the time. I knew that we were under attack. The order had gone out that all firemen were to report to duty. All leaves and vacations were canceled. We knew that the Pentagon had already been hit by a plane before we had left the fire house. In the meantime, Lieutenant Di Martino spoke to our crew about our duties upon arrival. We were a crew of 5. During the Lieutenant's briefing he informed us that many people would die, and that some would be firemen.

As we were in Manhattan headed for the Trade Center we could see both buildings on fire, and the South Tower as it started to collapse.

As we arrived to our location by the North Tower we saw a cloud of dust and debris. People were screaming. Fire radios were blaring, communicating about people being trapped. It was total chaos!

We were parked close to the North Tower. The company grabbed as much equipment as we could and ran into the North Tower. At that time, we were told by the members that had survived the South Tower attack that the Chief had ordered everyone to back off and head for safety. We were standing outside by the North Tower waiting for the next order, constantly looking up, due to the debris that was falling, and the people that were jumping.

Then the North Tower started to collapse. Those were 100 story buildings, and you could hear each floor collapsing; **Boom! Boom! Boom!** About one every second.

Everybody started running north, which seemed to be the safest route, while at the same time looking back over your shoulder to see how close the collapse was getting to you. At the point where I realized that I could not outrun everything that was flying and falling I positioned myself against the AT&T building hoping to make myself as small as possible between the sidewalk and the building. It was "duck and cover." At that time a civilian crouched in beside me. I put him under me and laid on top of him to protect him. It was an instinctive act as a fireman. Then I took my fireman's coat and trapped as much air inside as I could and covered us both. All the while I was thinking of my wife and children, and praying the Lord's Prayer and the 23rd psalm; at least the 1st three verses. That was all that would come to my mind at the time.

We were completely covered in darkness and debris. All the air was gone. I thought it was "lights out" for me. That period of no air lasted about a minute or so, but it seemed like an eternity. Then it started to go from black to gray and there was some air after that. It got a little lighter and I stood up. The civilian under me, Richard, thanked me and started to running toward the north.

Lieutenant Di Martino appeared and we ran back to the North tower to help those that were trapped. That is the way of fireman and first responders. We run toward danger while others run away. We didn't have to run far before we saw victims; those who were trapped, but still alive.

About fifteen minutes into the rescue no one still knew what was going on. Were we still under attack? Were we going to be attacked again? In the mean time we were busy trying to rescue people and suppress the fire.

We could hear the sound of fighter jets overhead in attack

mode. Some of the firemen working with me got up to start to run for cover again. I told them to come back, that those planes were ours, protecting us. One fellow said, "How do you know?" I said, "Because they couldn't get here." I knew that they would be shot down before they got to us. You could hear the F-14s but you could not see them. I was saying "thank you Jesus" and we continued our work of rescue and suppressing of fires.

My company stayed on duty until 11:30 that evening, and they sent us back to our Fire house. Around 12:30 I got to the fire house and finally called Debbie, and that was the first time that she knew that I was still alive.

For the past 15 years I have been receiving extensive medical treatments with a limited amount of success. I am alive! Three hundred and forty-three firemen died. I am blessed to have been able to see my children grow up. I recently became a grandfather; something I thought I would never do.

One of the firefighter's mottos is "Never give up! Never surrender." That is a motto from our Military that goes back to the Revolutionary war. Knowing that you have a family to defend and protect, and fellow fire fighters that depend on you to be there it keeps you going till your job is completed.

I strongly believe that anyone who does this work must have faith. I have faith, and my faith is in Jesus Christ.

RALPH

RALPH MURRAY WAS the first person I interviewed who attended the Pleasant Grove United Methodist Church in Peach Bottom Pa. where I was appointed as Interim Pastor. I chose to ask Ralph for an interview because I found him to be a very interesting person, had grown up in the area and had been civically involved to a very significant degree. I soon learned that Ralph was a distant relative on my father's side of the family. He was also the first and only African American member of the church. He and his wife Betty had joined under my leadership.

"I joined the church on the same day when the Second World War started. I was ten years old then. I joined the Arcadia AME church. Dad came to the tea party. He couldn't stay long. He had to go for guard duty on one of the tunnels. We were at Phoebe Wilson's house in Peach Bottom. After church we would have little tea parties. Arcadia was what the area was called. It was a little Black village.

The next day I was hospitalized with a ruptured appendix at Lancaster General. I have often wondered about that. Two things happened about the same time.

My grandfather was a Deacon, and my uncle Fred Dorsey told me that when I went to church I should always give the Lord my best.

I remember that the minister Thomas Wilson and his wife walked 3 miles to church. He was a butcher on Saturdays and he preached on Sundays. Three people strongly influenced my church life; Uncle Fred, Deacon Dunsen and Rev. Thomas Wilson. I always had an inclination toward the Lord. I was low key. I never expressed myself much, but I always knew what the Lord was doing for me. I knew for myself that I had the Lord in my heart.

From 1949 to 1953 I went to Lincoln University and graduated with a degree in Communication. I had good marks but I could not get in White Colleges. My grandmother convinced me to go to college. She did day work for farmers after my Grandfather passed away. My grandmother Bessie Clark Murray had a special way of dealing with problems. She would always say "well, we'll just pray about it.", and somehow the problems just seemed to be dissolved. She always promised to see me through. By that she meant that she would help me financially to get through college. I had a calf that I raised to sell every year to help pay my tuition.

Originally established as **The Ashmun Institute**, Lincoln University received its charter from the Commonwealth of Pennsylvania on April 24, 1854, making it the nation's first degree-granting Historically Black College and University (HBCU).

The story of Lincoln University dates back to the early years of the nineteenth century and to the ancestors of its founders, **John Miller Dickey**, and his wife, **Sarah Emlen Cresson**. The maternal grandfather of John Miller Dickey was a marble merchant in Philadelphia who made contributions to the education of African-Americans in that city as early as 1794. Dickey's father was a minister of the Oxford Presbyterian Church. After serving as a missionary and preaching to the slaves in Georgia, John Miller Dickey became pastor of that same church in Oxford, Pennsylvania, in 1832. Sarah Emlen Cresson inherited a long tradition of service and philanthropy through the Society of Friends in Philadelphia. John Miller Dickey was active in the American Colonization Society, and in 1851 took part in the court actions leading to the freeing of a young African-American girl who had been abducted from southern Chester County by slave raiders from Maryland. At the same time, having been unsuccessful in his efforts to gain college admission to even the most liberal of schools for a young freedman named James Amos, Dickey himself undertook to prepare the young man for the ministry.

In October 1853, the Presbytery of New Castle approved Dickey's plan for the establishment of "an institution to be called Ashmun Institute, for the scientific, classical and theological education of colored youth of the male sex."

In 1866, the institution was re-named **Lincoln University** in honor of President Abraham Lincoln. At that time, Dickey then proposed to expand the college into a full-fledged university and to enroll students of "every clime and complexion." Law, medical, pedagogical and theological schools were planned in addition to the College of Liberal Arts. White students were encouraged to enroll and two graduated in the first baccalaureate class of six men in 1868.[7]

Right out of college I entered military service. I had taken the ROTC course and became a sergeant, I entered at Fort Dix in New Jersey and joined the 9th infantry division. I had 8 weeks of basic training and then I went to Okinawa, Japan. On the ship going to Japan we hit a typhoon. Our vessel was the General Nelson Walker transport ship. It was a bad storm! It lasted about 7 or 8 hours. At 2 pm all of a sudden the storm rolled in. I heard a lot of fellows praying. The fellows who were used to using the worst language were the ones I heard praying the loudest. They knew that their lives were in danger. I had never seen men change so fast. I knew it was God's will. I said, the Lord will make a way somehow. The order was for all hands to go below deck. There were 3800 of us on that ship. I found a space and relaxed on my duffle bag. The night before we sailed three of us went to a Methodist church on Fillmore

---

[7] Information from the Lincoln University website

Street in San Francisco. You could stand in front of the church and see Alcatraz Island. The minister said that it was the first time that any military persons had come from the street to his church.

Today Jones Memorial United Methodist Church stands at approximately the same location in San Francisco. We all looked at the Golden Gate Bridge as we left it, wondering if we would ever see it again. Thirteen of the fellows I sailed with lost their lives. They were killed by what would be termed today as friendly fire. Four of us had played baseball together. We were members of an All Army Team. The Military was segregated at the time. I had gone from the first grade through high school in a mixed system. The first time that I faced segregation was in the Military. I never felt inferior or superior. I felt that we were all God's children. We went from Japan to Korea, and back to Japan. President Harry S. Truman was responsible for integrating the military services. He gave the Executive Order 9981 on July 26, 1948 desegregating the Armed Forces.[8]

On Saturday, September 27th, 2014 the following article written by Staff Writer Dave O'Connor appeared in the New Era Lancaster Newspaper with a picture of Ralph and his wife Betty. The article was titled **That's Dedication**.

What follows is an excerpt from that article;

This 83-year-old man is a Barnstormers fanatic. He's only missed two of the team's home games in its 10-year history. It's late on a warm, humid summer night in Lancaster, and on the field the baseball game is starting to drag.

The Lancaster Barnstormers have a big lead and fans are starting to head for the exits. But Ralph Murray hasn't even thought of getting up from his seat in Section 18 at Clipper Magazine Stadium and heading home. He continues to watch and keep score, a pleasant smile on his face. He and his wife Betty would rather be nowhere else.

Flash forward to this week, and it's a chilly evening at Lancaster's ball park for a playoff game.

---

[8] www.ourdocuments.gov/docphp?doc=84

And the 83-year-old Murray is there, just like he has been for all but two games in the Barnstormers' first 10 years. That means he's watched almost 700 games in the past decade.

"I enjoy watching the games. We enjoy the games, so we go to all of them." Murray of Fulton Township says this week, as the Barnstormers began their Atlantic League playoff series versus the Somerset Patriots.

The retired Lukens Steel Co. sales official might be the area's most dedicated fan, Barnstormer officials said.

"Ralph is a really special guy. There is a deep deep connection with Ralph and our team, our organization and our Stadium." said Tony DeMarco, the Barnstormer's vice president of fan experience.

Murray is a quietly knowledgeable fan DeMarco has noticed.

Ralph is quiet integrity, someone you can always count on, regardless of the weather. Every night, he'll ask me something like 'Are we going to get 'em tonight?' or, 'Is this our night?'

"Ralph is always optimistic, always the rainbow, not the rain." De Marco added.

Murray once ran track and played shortstop in his days at the former Quarryville High School, and he kept playing ball well into adulthood.

He became a Barnstormer fan after serving on the Lancaster County Redevelopment Authority, which helped bring the stadium and Lancaster's minor league team here.

He has come to love the team and many of its players, from former stars like Lance Burkhart and Reggie Taylor to current pitcher Scott Patterson.

"Once we started going as a family, I wanted to stay with it as long as I possibly could," Murray explained.

By saying "we" Murray isn't just being polite.

His wife, a retired licensed practical nurse from Conestoga View nursing home, is every bit the fan as her husband. Just like she grew up doing in Lexington, N.C. she keeps score at all of the Barnstormer games, also doing the same when the team's on the road and she's listening on the radio.

The Murrays, who both lost their first spouses and knew each other from when they all attended a Fulton Township church together, say they have a hobby they can share.

Ralph attributes his longevity, and every success to the goodness and mercy of God in his life. Ralph is an honest and honorable Christian man.

JANE

Mike Goad, his wife Jane, and their son Mike Edward first came to the Pleasant Grove church in January of 2011. They said that God had led them there.

I have found in that family a strong and genuine love for Christ and his church, and a sincere compassion for others. When I heard Jane expressing her faith I knew that it was authentic, and that her story needed to be told.

I was born in Portland, Oregon. We traveled to California, going first to Idaho. My great grandfather was with us until I was 5. My parents were migrants. We lived in our car. Mom had remarried. That is why we left Idaho. Dad would do day work; pick cotton, grape fruits, potatoes to get enough to get gas and food. Our destination was west; the west coast. We were not used to having a lot. We have also lived at the city dump, and on the river bank. I don't remember which state that was. When he married mom she had seven living children. He had a special heart. Mother was a poor woman. He was on the rodeo circuit. He met mom at a rodeo. It was all God's plan for our family. Dad would even stop and sell his blood to get food, and the day's needs.

We ended up in Seattle, Washington. We lived in Seattle for three years. Dad worked in the Lumber Yard. We lived in the Projects. We were helped by President Kennedy's Commodities Program, the early food stamp program.

Dad was born in Virginia. His mother named him Isaac. She said that it was because she laughed at the idea of getting pregnant again. The name Isaac is a Hebrew baby name. In Hebrew the meaning of the name Isaac is; he laughs, or laughter. According to the Old Testament Abraham laughed when God told him that his aged wife Sarah would become pregnant with Isaac (Genesis 17; 17.)

Mom and dad taught us survival; and we pass it on.

They taught us how to make do with what we had. They taught us how to wash pans with sand, brush our teeth with salt, and cook on open fire. When dad was working mom would read to us literature and funny tales. She kept us busy and entertained. We loved her presence, her voice, her facial expressions; we absorbed it all. She taught us to have manners; sit up straight and to be respectable. She passed on to us what was good and right. Her grandmother had instilled those virtues in her. While we were running around as vagabonds she was instilling those things in us; and she still does.

For four years we lived on a small farm on Vashon Island. We were living a normal life. We lived in a blue house that had white shutters, and a Chinese red ceiling in the kitchen. We even had a piano.

In 1966 daddy's brother passed away in Colora, Maryland. Most of his siblings were here. Mom and dad lived together for almost 40 years. He died a few days before their fortieth anniversary.

We had a big Ford Station Wagon. We took a small trailer with all our belongings and came here. There were six children, mom and dad, and a dog. One more was born in Havre De Grace; our baby. It took us seven days of traveling to get here. When we arrived we came to a very large Christian family.

I had gotten saved out on that Island, but I didn't make it public until I got here. I was baptized here. The family took us to Bible School. Little church buses would pick us up and we would go to church. After a week of Bible school, I left our house and went next door to the old berry field. The field was golden. There I accepted the Lord. I know it happened then. There was a field beside us that had berry vines that had dried up from the summer sun; and the grasses grew up and turned yellow, and were swaying in the little wind. I felt God's presence. I knew that I was not out there alone.

Daddy's people were a lovely Christian family. Daddy's nieces and nephews were all a part of Conowingo Baptist, and another Pentecostal Church. They all had a deep burden for our family, and were very supportive. Dad had two brothers that were Christians. It was the children of the brother that passed away who carried the mantle to make sure that my daddy was eternally secure, and passed it right on to us.

At his brother's funeral Daddy heard a reading from the 14th chapter of John. That comforted him, knowing that God was real.

My daddy was 14 when his mom died, and at the age of 15 he was in the Navy at Bainbridge NTC. The preacher verified that he was of age. He was in the Normandy Invasion, and received a medal for that three weeks before he passed away. (October 2,000, Nov 13th 2000)

Back when I was 5, Daddy took us into Seattle to a Sunrise Service in and Amphitheater. We were in the back looking down. What I saw was the celebration of Easter. That to me was holy! Mom let us go on the bus to a Christmas program. I was 6. I remember the angels, and the baby in the manger. It was so beautiful! I felt like I was experiencing a part of Heaven. I knew it was the hand of God bringing Daddy into our lives!

Three or four months' earlier mom had divorced my birth father. Daddy and mom met in the potato field. He was driving the truck, and she was on the conveyor belt, and that's how they met. September and October was the time of the potato harvest. Off we went packed in our car with our beloved great grandfather's blessing, and my birth father in the Penn in Boise, Idaho.

I believe from the Scriptures that God forgives sins. I

know that He has forgiven my sins. I believe in heaven. Mom and my birth father's first two children died at 7, and 12 months. Mom told us that Ramona and Johnny were in heaven, and that we would see them again. That is what gave her comfort; and us too.

The first time that I learned that God forgives sins was in that Bible school at age 11. I learned that Jesus died on that cross and washed me white as snow. That is the way God saw me after that. I have a very child-like faith, because I go back to where I first believed. I have come a long way, but I'll never forget the place where God started me out as a child.

All of my siblings came to a saving knowledge of Christ. We work hard at holding each other up, through struggles. We are all on that mission to save souls. There is forgiveness when we fall and when we fail. We are picked up by that unconditional love of God in Christ, in our family.

God is at work in my life. He brought Mike to me. I know it was God's hand. It happened a week after graduation from High School. I had just gotten out of the 9th grade. My old boyfriend and I had just broken up. He drowned a year later at Muddy Run. I thought he was the one for me. A year and 7 months later Mike and I had never been out on a date before. I was 15 when Daddy found out who he was. He let me go out with him. Six months after we started dating Mike signed up to go into the Air Force. I thought I could not take another loss. I tried to take my life by taking 16 mellarills. God saved my life. I have never tried that again. Temptation comes, but I never had that to bear with again. I have never taken drugs, and only drank a half of a beer in my life.

Concentrating on losses caused negative thinking; Ramona and Johnny, my birth father, my great grandfather, my ex-boyfriend- etc. Learning the truth in the scriptures, singing hymns. All that gives me hope. I have enjoyed Christian music from a teen-ager up. That has been a great part of my life.

At Conowingo Baptist Church I was a member of the G A's the Girls Auxiliary. That's where we studied world missions and the Scriptures. I loved all those great hymns in the Baptist hymnal.

Mike and I got married in the Parsonage of the Conowingo Baptist church, and there was a spiritual turning point in my life on 9/1/76 God is God. Nothing and nobody else. No messing around. I was 7 months pregnant and had been married for 4 years. Mike was out of the Air Force. We had a home in Rising Sun. We thought everything was normal. We were both working, and we were going to have a family. But I was born with a double womb, (and mom lost baby # 4 and baby # 5 out of 12 children.)

I woke up one morning at 5:00am in labor. He was born in our bed. I never thought he would die. It was very traumatic. The doctor told me to call an ambulance. He followed behind the ambulance. They took me into the hospital. I heard the nurses talking. They said "This is a dirty baby." That meant that he had not been born in the hospital under sterile conditions. They called him a monster. It was a medical expression for a newborn that did not appear as normal. Our first baby was a miscarriage, an emaciated monster. My second child, Michael Leonard lived for two and a half hours. He was born, and passed away on September the 1st, 1976. He was 28 weeks old and weighted an estimated 3 pounds. We had only a graveside service for him.

Michael Leonard's life was not in vain because he is part of our treasures in heaven. I had to learn to accept God's will. It is precious what I have learned from his little gift of life. I have truly accepted God's will, and I know I'll see him.

Knowing Jesus we are never alone. He is the answer to every problem that we have. Knowing Him is full joy, fulfillment, and peace that passes understanding, and that is a mystery.

When we bought our land I asked God to fill it up with children if it was his will, although the Doctors had told us that we would never have children.

Megan and Holly are biological sisters. They were born a year apart. Holly was born in March of 1978, and Megan was born in March of 1979. They were 3 and 4 years old when we learned about them. Three weeks from the time we learned about them the adoption was official.

Fifteen years later Michael Edward came along. Michael Edward Goad. His name was actually Megan's nick name, MEG. We did that on purpose. We had full custody of Michael Edward for four years, then we adopted him.

I think what is most important in life is learning to trust God's word, his promises to meet our deepest needs and desires. His Word becomes so necessary! It is food! There is peace because you know that God is working it all out. I took the doctors off the pedestal and put God in their place because I know that they didn't have the power. I had been inaccurate in my thinking because I thought the doctors had all the answers. But I have discovered that God is the answer. We just need belief, patience, and trust. God's word tells us that he is working all things out for our good. Romans 8; 28 is one example. It says "For we know that all things work together for good for those who love the Lord, for those who are called according to his purpose."

At a point of great frustration, I had run to my Pastor's house crying. I said, "I just can't take it anymore!" The Pastor's wife took time and prayed with me. Two weeks later we got the word about the girls.

The most important thing is to know our Lord Jesus, one on one, as Savor and Lord. It is never too late to know that He cares for every area of our lives. We are never alone. It is unspeakable joy to have that peace, comfort, and unconditional love. That is when we have true fulfillment as humans. To pass this message along is the most awesome heritage that you can give to your children.

RON

RON AND BERTHA Weaver were two of the many supportive couples that I have found at the church. Bertie even told me about a vision she had about the first African American to be the Pastor of Pleasant Grove.

Many churches go through struggles that challenge their ability to survive. A few years ago Ron stepped in at a crucial time in the life of the church during economic times. I was impressed by his story and thought it needed to be shared.

"I was brought up about three quarters of a mile from the church. It was early on that I realized that prayer worked. It was in 1954. Dad was from Harford County. We were on our way to Harford County on a long trip and the car stopped. I prayed that the car would start, and it did. I was 10 years old then. I really prayed hard. I thought we would never get home again. I just believed that prayer worked. I was scared too. We were a long way from home. I felt like my prayer helped. After the car started we turned around and came back. Every now and then I think about that. When I wonder about praying for somebody my mind goes back there. I always said prayers at night. Mom made us do it. She didn't whip us to make us do it but she would ask us if we did. We lived in Arcadia for a few years, and went to a little church there; an African Methodist church. We knew everybody because we all went to the same school together.

For years I quit going to church. I worked 7 days a week so my wife would not have to. She took care of the kids.

Growing up I found work on neighborhood farms. Back then I was earning five dollars a week. I went to work at the Bata Shoe factory in 1961. There I started making a dollar and forty cents an hour, working forty hours a week. Later I went to work in the stone quarry earning the same amount per hour, but I worked nearly 80 hours a week. When I worked there at night I was paid a dollar and fifty cents an hour. Later I went to work at Wiley's ship yard in Port Deposit. My job was welding. I had learned forge welding when I was 12 years old. Forge welding is joining two pieces of metal by heating them to a high temperature and then hammering them together.

I liked metal work because of Grandad, being a Blacksmith. He was my mom's dad, William Douglas. He was not big but he was muscular. He worked until he was in his 80s. He encouraged me. He said, "If a job is worth doing it is worth doing to the best of your ability. I didn't make money working with him; just the experience. He was a good craftsman.

At the stone quarry I had gotten into welding more. At Wiley's Ship yard I worked as a tacker. Tacking is joining pieces of metal with a number of small welds spaced apart. Tack welding requires a certain amount of practice.

I worked there until 1964, becoming a first class welder. I worked for CC Welding earning four dollars an hour, left in 1970 earning six dollars an hour. I became self-employed and traveled to Texas, Missouri, Kansas and Mississippi. On May 11th 2007 I retired from Johnston Construction Company as a General Superintendent. At that time, I was earning forty-eight dollars an hour plus Bonuses.

It was a unique rural area that we grew up in. Nobody moved except when looking for work. It was a close community, and the church was the center piece of the community; the church and the store porch. The guys would meet and tell stories on Fry's grocery store porch in town. We didn't know, that I can recall, about racial problems until recently. We heard about it on the news. I had a buddy. His name was Early Smith. We played in the sand box together. There was a boy named G. Lewis. He was from the South. He asked me if I knew that Early was a Nigger. So I asked Early if he was a Nigger. He said that he didn't know but that he would ask his mother. Early's mother worked with my mom. That next night I got one of the worse thrashings I got in my life. I couldn't understand all the confusion at the time. Mom taught me that you have to respect everybody. I think about that and feel bad. Boy! I wish I hadn't asked Early that. The next day we were in the sand box again. I have never let society influence me from the way I grew up.

People came from the south to work on farms, or on the Conowingo Dam etc. There are not a lot of people here now that were here when I grew up. Modernization caused farmers to need less hands; less work.

There was no crime, racial divide, nothing serious. Everybody was on the same level. You couldn't break into your neighbor's house and steal something because what you didn't have he didn't have either.

Jesus Christ is the Son of God. He is the Savior of all people. It is the security that you have, knowing that there is a God and that you can have a better life. Some of the jobs I've had; some of the places I've had to get into and get out—I had a prayer in my heart at all times. It is a comfort to know that you will someday be in heaven. It hurt a lot of people taking prayer out of schools. The only prayer some children had was in school. Now there is no right or wrong. You can't say follow your heart because the heart has been corrupted by society. You could say, "Be like your grandfather" but as years go by that will change too. You should live your life so you can make your family proud of you. That can bring everything back into perspective. The only way you can do that is to use the Bible as a guide book for your life. Even if you are not religious if you follow the Bible it is good for humanity's sake; not just your sake. The Ten Commandments is a good place to start. That's the way a person should live. Get as close to Jesus as you can. Have respect for yourself, and other people too.

So for years I didn't go to church but I still believed. I never traveled much. Going to Lancaster was a big deal. The local store had all we needed. The store keeper could tell the size sock you wore by wrapping it around your fist. In the 60's things got better, but small stores died out.

As a kid, if you did something wrong the Lord would strike you. The Lord would punish you. If he didn't your mother would. Grandfather Douglas would say, "There is a supreme being. If you live like the Bible tells you, you'll have a good life. I believed that, and I thought it was a guide book for proper life. You didn't always get what you wanted but you got what you needed.

Yes; I spent years not going to church; partly because of work, and partly because I just didn't care. My wife and family went. I thought that was good enough. But there was a preacher, the Rev. Thomas Barniger who kept coming and pestering me. One day he came around. I was drinking a beer. I was tired, and hot, had been working all day. I really didn't want to be bothered. So I said, "If you drink a beer with me I'll go to church." He said, "I believe you're an honest man, and you mean what you say." So he drank a beer with me that day, and the next day I want to church. That was 40 years ago. I have never stopped going to church since.

One experience I will never forget. During real cold days the church furnace wouldn't start. I had to go in there early and press the reset button so there would be heat for service. I remember one day I was complaining about having to do that. When I left the church and went back to my car I saw a man walking toward the church door. He had burlap bags around his feet and an arm load of kindling wood. He carried the kindling wood into the church. To me that was saying, "Quit griping!" You got it easy! That was scary and embarrassing! That was the way they did it before the oil furnace. When I told my wife about it she asked me if I was day dreaming. I said, "No! That was real! I couldn't see his face because it was covered because of the weather. One thing for sure, I didn't gripe any more. I got a happy attitude instead. That was not a punishment, but a correction of my attitude. I will never forget that experience, or the car prayer.

There were several different times when we couldn't afford a preacher. Heating oil and electric were expensive. We did what we could to keep the church going. We had to buy oil a couple of times. When we didn't have a preacher I would preach. I'm not a good speaker, but if you pray the Lord will get you through it. We would have a preacher off and on for about three years. We got a little ahead because we didn't have to pay a preacher. I was scared to death up there, but I knew God was with me. I was told to preach from the Bible and I would be ok. I enjoyed it, especially when it was over. The people were happy. We grew some then; not much, but enough to keep the doors open. I don't know why I preached; didn't want the church to close, and there was nobody else. I don't know why I did it. Looking back, I'm glad I did what I did. I also did a lot of the maintenance. It was hard but satisfying. We were working against great odds. We called ourselves the "can do gang."

We probably should have failed. But by God's Grace and Blessing, we didn't fail.

An Ordinary Woman from Africa

LIFE HAS BEEN quite a challenge for Loretta McCrae who was born in Ghana, West Africa. Loretta came from a divided family. Her mom and dad divorced not long after her birth. She left, living with her maternal grandmother and went to live with her dad and her older sister. Loretta resented her stepmother at first. Her step mother was eight years younger than her dad. Her father's family was not close at all. She had been named after her paternal grandmother whom she never knew. Her grandmother had been the most educated person in the family. This caused some friction. Her father's family was Episcopal, and her mother's family was Methodist. Loretta remembers that her father would visit three or four times a year. He lived eighty-eight miles away... But he did come and would go to church. He would sit in the pew that belonged to his family. If someone else happened to be sitting in his pew when he arrived, the ushers would be obliged to ask them to move.

Loretta's mom remarried and had two sons. The marriage, however, did not last. Her mother ended up joining the military. Loretta describes her mom as being a simple person who was carefree. As she saw it, her dad's family tried to be sophisticated. Loretta remembers that there were financial difficulties. There were many days, she recalls, that they barely had food. The public schools were good, but she was taken out of school many times because of financial problems. On two occasions she was taken out of school for almost a year and she had no homeschooling during those times. It was said about her father that he "hung his hat where his hand could not reach." He always lived above his means.

Loretta was in the first grade when her father came to the U.S. His plan was send for them, but he never did. Loretta's stepmother took care of her and her sister until they were adults. Her mother's family did not want the children around because the father had left, and they didn't think that the stepmother should have the responsibility for the children. Loretta was wrongfully blamed for a lot of things, and was mistreated to the extent that she wanted to give up on life. Many things had been done to belittle her because of family rivalry.

In school corporal punishment was practiced. Loretta recalls a horrible time in her life when she was in the ninth grade. She said, "I was programmed to fail at everything! I was beaten so badly that I spent two days in the hospital. I was angry at life and angry at everybody." She said that someone close to the family attempted to molest her on several occasions. She recalls having been taken to a nightclub against her will. She had suffered unspeakable abuse. A family friend attempted to get her intoxicated so that he could carry out his plan to molest her, but his plan failed. Some of the treatment that Loretta received really defies description; therefore, she was virtually ready to give up on life itself. She also spent some time living in a Refugee camp.

But there was a girl in Loretta's class whose name is Alice. There was nothing that anyone could do that would make Alice angry. She went to Alice to talk to her and tried to find out where she got her tremendous strength. Alice told her that it was Christ who was in her life and that He was the one who changed her life. Alice also told Loretta that Christ could change her life as well. So, Loretta believed Alice and prayed, saying, "Jesus, if you're really there I want you to change my life. I want peace and joy in my life." Two days later Loretta's mother came to get her. Her stepmom had also accepted Christ. The rest of the family also began to experience the joy that Loretta knew. She knew that there was a lot of unrest and abuse. Loretta prayed again, "God, help me to help other young women. I want to be the voice for those who cannot speak for themselves." Loretta had, for some time, resented her dad's Aunt who had been abusive to her in the past. In fact, she wished her evil, and had wanted to kill her. After her encounter with Christ, the resentment and evil desires disappeared.

Soon, Loretta began to have daily prayer and Bible study

with her mother. They discussed daily activities, sang traditional choruses and hymns, and spent much quality time together. In high school she started a Bible study during recess time. Some of the students called her Mother Theresa, Holy Mary, etc. She felt good about reaching out to lower income children; to the less fortunate children. She also became a Motivational Speaker for the World Student Christian Federation. Once in 1990, when she was visiting a refugee camp, Loretta saw a young woman who was very beautiful, but she was very ill. She said to herself, "Who is this woman?" That day God spoke to her and told her to write to the woman; so she wrote a three-page note and gave it to her. In her note she told her that even though she didn't know who she was, there was hope. Loretta quoted several Scriptures about faith, hope, and the love of God. When she went back to the camp the next day, the woman was not there.

After some time, one day in 1994 when Loretta was getting ready to come to the United States to continue her education, she walked into a store to make a purchase. The woman walked up to her and identified herself. She said, "I am the one you met in the refugee camp. I was contemplating suicide. I read your letter, and remembered that my mother had told me about God. I prayed and read the passages that you had written, and I prayed and asked the God in whom my mother believed to come to my rescue. I got out, finished college, and now I work for the United States Embassy. Thank you for saving my life."

Although she has faced many additional challenges in her life, Loretta has grown considerably in her faith in God and her commitment to Jesus Christ. She was successful in a determined effort to educate herself. Although a failed marriage was for her a setback, she refused to accept defeat. She has become an effective ordained pastor in a major Christian denomination in the United States. Loretta says, "In this world there is too much hate, and too much desire to conquer and control. There are no superior or inferior people. God created us in God's image. Somewhere in each of us is a sense of God. Seek to be at peace with the one thing that makes us the same. We are all in the image and likeness of God. Jesus came to unite us and show us love. I used to have resentment. But now I can't find it! I have experienced divine forgiveness. I am free! I don't think I can find it within myself to hate, or take vengeance. I used to, but not now!"

An Ordinary Man

THE REVEREND DAVID Nissley, Pastor of the Lampeter United Methodist Church in Lancaster County, Pennsylvania, befriended us and welcomed us to the church. It was his wife Linda who invited us to have a tour of the Northeast Regional Office of the Wycliffe Organization. Linda was the Housing Coordinator, caring for missionaries who were on furlough.

I had heard of Wycliffe Bible Translators before, but the tour sparked my interest to a significant degree. I wanted to learn more. My inquiry led me immediately to Uncle Cam.

William Cameron Townsend was born into poverty on July 9th, 1896 in Eastville, a settlement near Los Angeles, California. Although times were extremely hard, his father Will was a stubborn, determined man who never seemed to give up. He was known for his deep-seated honesty and his hard work philosophy. Mr. Townsend was very strict on his two boys; whenever they did sloppy work, he would insist that they do it over until it became second nature to them. Cam and his younger brother Paul were strongly influenced by their father's strictness and seriousness and by their mother's cheerfulness. Molly kept the house happy with flowers, and laughing and joking with the children.

The members of the Townsend family read large portions of the Bible daily, beginning before milking every morning and ending with devotions after breakfast. Through his father's influence Cam came into a personal relationship with Jesus Christ at the age of twelve.

Despite financial challenges the family faced, he managed to graduate from high school with the highest average in the class. During high school years Cam dreamed of someday learning to fly, and until his last year planned to become a teacher. He was particularly challenged by the life and witness of Hudson Taylor, founder of the China Inland

Mission. It was Taylor's faith, his pioneering spirit, and his adaptation to life in China that held Cam's attention. He longed for a call from God to be a missionary. He thought that if he received such a call, he would become a man like Mr. Taylor.

In January, 1917, Cam learned that the Bible House of Los Angeles was recruiting Bible salesmen to work in South America. Since he had studied Spanish in high school, and some College Spanish, he decided to apply. His plan was to work for a year in Central America, then return and finish college. The Bible Company approved his application and assigned him to Guatemala. His family was disappointed because they thought he would never return to finish college. Cameron panicked because he had a commitment to the National Guard. Congress declared war in April of that year, and he was certain that he would not be able to go south.

However, through a remarkable series of events, William Cameron Townsend was relieved of his responsibility to the military, freeing him to go to sell bibles in South America. The captain agreed to his discharge, and gave him a word of encouragement, saying that he would accomplish much more by selling bibles in Central America than he would by shooting Germans in France. Cameron and his friend spoke to Stella Zimmerman, a seasoned missionary who had spent more than a dozen years in Guatemala, who told them a great deal about the country and about being a missionary.

Cam and his friend Robby Robinson worked hard at a Wells Fargo warehouse in San Francisco to earn the money to pay their own fare, since that was the only way they would be able to go. They sailed out of the San Francisco Bay on September 15th, 1917, and arrived in Guatemala eighteen days later.

Cameron and Robby learned a lot about their new world in a very short time. One thing that they learned was that the indigenous peoples did not speak Spanish well at all, and that it would be very difficult, if not impossible, to introduce them to Jesus Christ. After all, Cam and Robby's most important responsibility, as they understood it, was to bring the message of salvation to the people of Guatemala. But if language was such a problem, how would they witness to the Indians?

Since arriving in the country they had learned that the Indians were marginalized people. An American traveler had informed them that in Guatemala, if you are wanted to be respected, it was necessary to be a person of Spanish descent. One could pretend to be of Spanish descent by speaking the language perfectly. It soon became clear to them that the Indians were regarded as the least and the lowest in Guatemalan society. But there were many Indians in Guatemala.

Edward Bishop, director of Central American Mission Work was their contact with the Bible House back in the States. It was Mr. Bishop who assigned Robby and Cameron to their territories Cam was assigned to San Antonio Aguas Calientes, and Santa Catarina, where there existed a group of Cakchiquel Indian Christians. How did they get there?

There had been very few Cakchiquel Indians who could read and understand Spanish. One of them, Silverio Lopez, had bought a bible in Guatemala City when he had been working there. Finding it hard to understand, he put it away. Then, when he returned home, one of his children died, and another became gravely ill. According to the witch doctor, the problems in his family were caused by the spirits of dead ancestors, and he should buy candles and put them before an image in a local church. Between the cost of the candles and the fee for the seer Silverio ended up deeply in debt. But one day Silverio found scrap of paper on the road. Written on it were the words, "My Father's house should be called a house of prayer, but you have made it a den of thieves." When he got home, he looked up the verse in his bible, decided to stop paying the witch doctor, bought medicine from the drug store for his daughter, and she got well. Shortly thereafter Silverio Lopez received Christ as his Savior. That had been six months before Cam heard the story. Since that time Silverio had led forty Indians to Christ.

Although Cameron Townsend had intended to be in Guatemala for only one year to sell bibles and then return to college, his stay was extended to fifteen months. During that time, he and his friend Robby survived a tragic earthquake and the after-shock was equally as tragic as the initial quake. He had also carried his bible to isolated areas of four countries in Central America. He had to make a decision. Would he return or would he stay? He had mixed feelings because he knew his family would be disappointed if he did not return. He had made a public commitment to become an ordained minister of the Gospel, which would require him to finish college and then go to Seminary. But there was so much need in Guatemala! He had been living with the Cakchiquel Indians and was starting to learn their language. He saw their needs, but also their possibilities. He was persuaded that God wanted him to remain there. He was happy to get his mother's approval. She said that he should do only God's will. His father was also supportive of his decision.

Meanwhile Cam's heart was burdened for the Cakchiquel Indians. He wanted to build a school for them and to put their language into written form. His plan was to translate the Holy Scriptures into the heart language of the people. But, first, he had to learn the language. It was a long and tedious challenge. He did get some helpful advice from Dr. Gates, an Archaeologist traveling in the area. Dr. Gates told him about a descriptive approach to learning a primitive type of language, essentially, trying to learn and understand the language well in its own form and with its own characteristics without imposing any structural model. Dr. Gates also put Cam in contact with an ethnologist from the University of Chicago and also sent him valuable writings. Cameron Towsend's task was tremendous! He would also need to teach the people to read their language, once it was written.

His first attempt at translating the Bible was the Gospel of Mark, which would take him ten years to complete. It would be a bilingual production with Cakchiquel on one page and Spanish on the opposite page. Since the people would learn to read their language, and then learn to read Spanish, the authorities were supportive and facilitated the printing of the first four chapters. That portion of the book was produced and well received by the people. "Look! Look! God speaks our language!" could be heard often as the news of the new book was shared.

Cameron's work was not easy; success was mixed with tragedy and criticism. By the time he had spent eight years in the mountains of Guatemala, he had built a clinic, taught carpentry to the Indians, given them agricultural help, established a printing press, and built schools, a bible institute and chapels in many villages. He had observed that Christianity helped the Indians' self-esteem, as they learned to read their language and learned the Word of God. But his friend Robby had died from a hemorrhage. Three of his closest friends had died, and his wife Elvira was suffering from emotional problems and heart trouble. He had not reached the age of thirty and he was thinking of his own mortality. But Cam was encouraged by the story of the life of Lazarus in the eleventh chapter of the Gospel of John. "Jesus said, 'I am the resurrection and the life. Whoever believes in me, though he die, yet shall he live.'" Cam told his wife that the Word of God was the only thing that made any sense.

Cameron's emphasis on helping the Indians, especially when the translation work was called into question by some of the members of the Central American Mission organization, which was responsible for his work in Guatemala. But he was able to justify his position by his successful evangelism among the indigenous people, his strong theological position, and the Word of the Lord. He reasoned that since the Bible said that every nation would bow to the King of Kings, and that every knee should bow and that every tongue should confess that Jesus Christ is Lord, that must include the Cakchiquels, as he saw it, there were nearly five hundred thousand to a million Cakchiquels in Guatemala who needed the Word of God in their own language. Cam believed that "God translated the human heart out of the power of Satan into the power of God through the Word of God in whom we have redemption, through the blood of Jesus, even the forgiveness of sins." Cam also wanted to use the Word of God to set the Indians free from vice and superstition and move them to more dignity and a better quality of life.

On the 19th of May, 1931, the first celebration of the New Testament in the Cakchiquel language took place in the Presidential Palace. The chief guest was the Chief Executive of the country; the President of the Republic of Guatemala. He received the first copy, which was leather-bound. The next day a dedication was made in the mountains, in an area where most of the translation work had been done and completed. The most memorable moment for Cam was when a complete stranger walked up to him and said, "This is wonderful! God speaks our language!"

Several months later Cam and his wife met a special traveler. He was a public education official of the government of Mexico, a leader in the Ministry of Education. He was deeply concerned about the education and wellbeing of indigenous groups in his country. In a later conversation, he invited Cam to bring his expertise to Mexico, saying that there were many more tribes there and many more languages that had never been written. That Mexican official would be instrumental in helping Cameron to enter Mexico and begin his translation work there in the future.

Later, Cameron Townsend received a letter of invitation from the University of Mexico to come and begin work toward creating a written language for the 50 tribes there who as yet did not have the Word of God in their language of the soul. He had accomplished a major work in Guatemala. He was encouraged by the letter from the University, and by the biblical story in Luke 14; 4 about the Ninety and Nine, to take his expertise to Mexico. It was now 1932. The Cakchiquels had the New Testament in their own language, they had the Holy Spirit, and they did not need the Townsends to stay and supervise them.

In early 1933 after seeing the doctor about a persistent cough. Both Cam and Elvira were ordered back to the United States, and both were ordered to be on bed rest. They spent time in Chicago recuperating where Elvira's family lived and where they had spent time before.

While they were in Chicago they met an old Preacher friend who had worked with the Comanche Native Americans and had been to the Amazon Basin. He too was interested in Mexico and reminded them that there were still 50 tribes in Mexico who did not have the Bible in their own language. Since it had taken the better part of 13 years to complete the work on the New Testament in the Cakchiquel language, they knew they would not have the time or the energy to make an impact in Mexico. They needed a new approach, a new strategy. Their doctor released Cam and Elvira to go to Mexico for a visit, but Elvira soon became too ill to go. The trip to Mexico was a success, but when Cam returned to Chicago, he found his wife ill again. They moved to Sulphur Springs, Arkansas. In 1934, when Cam couldn't return to Guatemala, and he did not yet have the permission to return to Mexico, he decided to create the Summer Institute of Languages to train some translators to carry on the work.

They only had two students on that first summer at the Wycliffe camp, named after the Englishman who first translated the Scriptures into English. They started in a borrowed barn, sitting on borrowed nail kegs from a hardware store, a humble, rustic beginning. The next summer, in 1935 they had a total of five students. Those five were the original members of what eventually became known as Wycliffe Bible Translators.

It was later in 1935 that the Townsends were permitted by the Mexican government to go to Mexico to continue their work. There they were welcomed by Mexican authorities to investigate the Indian languages, to create a means of writing them, and to share with them the Word of God.

They settled in an ancient Aztec village, Tetelcingo. Their work was to write down the language, to teach the people to read, and to translate the Bible into the new written language. Cameron Townsend began with the Aztec language; writing it down, and teaching the people to read in both Aztec and Spanish. Mexican President Cárdenas welcomed Cam, but asked him not to be involved in the country's politics. He said that the Church would be allowed to do its work if it would stay out of politics. From that time on, it has been the policy of the Wycliffe Bible Translators to cooperate with the government of the countries where they live and work. The Wycliffe Bible Translators have also continued to help the people in practical ways, following the example of Jesus who "came not to be served, but to serve, and to give his life for others."

The third Summer Linguistics Institute was held in 1936. There were more than fourteen students, one of whom was Eugene Nida, who would someday direct the translation program of the American Bible Society. President Cárdenas gave Cam permission to bring many new linguists to live and work among the people as long as they would follow the example laid down by Cameron himself.

As the work of translation expanded, it became more and more evident that a formal organization was needed. Therefore, Cameron and his friends and associates organized and elected a Field Committee that would be responsible for making policy, assignment and location of translation work, and accountability. That would be the work of the Summer Linguistics Institute. It would be the first agency ever established for the purpose of writing down languages that had not been previously written, and translating the Bible into every language.

Of the some 5,100 languages spoken in our world today it is estimated that nearly 3,000 still need to be written down. Wycliffe Bible Translators employs over 4000 employees, and is in need of more than 1,000 additional people in technical and non-technical fields. [9]

"It was because he believed wholeheartedly in God's goodness that Uncle Cam was able to dream impossible dreams and to see them come true. It was because Uncle Cam believed in God's goodness that he was able to become a pioneer in carrying out the task of Bible translation. Because he believed in the goodness of the Lord, Cameron Townsend was able to see countless lives renewed by reading the Word of God in their own language. Because of his faith in God,

---

[9] Much of the information about Uncle Cam and his work was extracted from materials supplied by Wycliffe Bible Translators, and a book called Uncle Cam, by James and Marti Hefley.

Uncle Cam laughed at what people called impossible, and declared, "It shall be done!"

An Ordinary Farm Girl from California

I FIRST MET Joanne Shetler at the Lampeter United Methodist Church in Lancaster County, in Pennsylvania. The church has a great burden for missions and supports many missionaries and mission projects. Missionaries who are either home on furlough or are visiting in the area make special presentations during the morning worship service. Joanne had come to talk about the successful completion of the translation of the New Testament into the language of the Balangao people of the Philippines. I was impressed by her presentation and joined her that same afternoon for a subsequent presentation at a Missions Fair at the nearby Smoketown Airport.

After her presentation at the Missions Fair I asked for permission to interview her. She said that her schedule was really tight, but that I could do it if I was willing to go to the JAARS Center near Waxhaw, North Carolina. JAARS stands for "Jungle Aviation and Radio Service." JAARS provides quality technical support and services for the Wycliffe Bible Translators.

My wife, Margie and I did drive to JAARS the following

week. Waxhaw is located near the South Carolina border. Actually, in order to arrive in Waxhaw, North Carolina we had to pass through a small town in South Carolina. We spent the night there, and I interviewed Jo Shetler the next day after lunch.

Jo grew up as a German farmer's daughter. It was not fun, but she had a good home. It was an authoritarian situation her father had never received real nurturing, therefore he did not know how to give it. Jo's father loved his children. He was very strict on them and used corporal punishment to keep them in line. Her two brothers got punished. One of them got punished more for daydreaming and the other for not responding properly. Her father rarely had to hit Jo. He just yelled at her. Jo knew her father loved her, although he was not able to express it openly to her. Her mom told her so. Jo loved, respected, and feared her father. He could fix anything. Jo was an adult when she discovered that not all men could fix all things that ever broke. But Jo never really knew her dad, even as an adult. She recalls that there were no casual conversations with her father, but she could talk to her mother. She also recalls that he was a different person in public than he was at home. At home, she could not communicate with him; she was afraid of him.

Mr. Shetler suffered a major stroke at the age of eighty. According to Jo, one of the effects was that it completely changed his personality. She said, "It was as if a satanic stronghold had been removed."

Jo's dad was very honest, scrupulous, and he was a good provider. He was helpful to his neighbors. When there was a fire that destroyed a farm neighbor's home he ran a campaign to get the family back on their feet. The farm was a few miles away. Houses were far apart. The three children were allowed one hour on Saturdays to go and play with the nearest neighbors, walking for about a mile to get there.

There was lots of work. Jo's father worked very hard, as did everyone else in the family. Jo's mother was an R.N. Jo remembers lots of arguments (spats) about family needs. Her mom would provide those little extras for the children that their father thought were not necessary, such as the "nickel for an ice cream."

The first time Jo became aware of God was when she was a little child. When she looked up at the stars at night and saw them twinkle, she asked herself, "How does He do that?" As she listened to the crickets she concluded that perhaps God held the stars all on strings against a black velvet sky, and He shook them at night. They were probably like balls of tin foil and she could hear them twinkle. She was disappointed when she found out that the sound was coming from the crickets. She told herself that if someone could make the stars it would have to be God. Authority was a very real part of Jo's life. She reasoned, "With the hierarchy there's got to be the top; and that had to be God."

Jo always felt awkward and out of place at school because she was tall, her hair was straight, and she wore feed-sack dresses. She and her brothers always had to take the bus home right after school because of the farm work that had to be done.

But at age 10 something happened to Jo that would change her life forever. She heard that God offered forgiveness for sins and eternal life to those who would ask Him. She said that her hand shot up when the Bible club teacher, the Child Evangelism teacher, asked those who wanted to accept Christ as their Savior to raise their hand. For Jo, that was really good news! She said that it was like discovering gold!

Although she had no trouble accepting the Bible as God's authoritative Word, she was troubled by the command to go into all the world and tell people about God. But one Sunday a missionary came to her church and spoke. From his message she understood that 90% of the people who go and tell the good news and make disciples were concentrating on only 10% of the world's population. When Jo heard that, she sat up in her seat. That meant that the other 10% of those who went out to spread the good news and make disciples had to reach 90% of the world. Right then and there Jo concluded that she was going to have to be a missionary, although she was not sure what that meant.

Jo's dad never was against the church. When she informed

him that she was interested in doing missionary work, possibly abroad his reply was that she could to that at home. In other words he didn't mind her doing mission work. He just didn't want her to leave. She was a very valuable worker. Her mom didn't want her to leave, either. She just had different reasons.

Although Jo had collected a lot of material, she still felt she had a very meager knowledge of what missionaries actually did. She was frightened at the prospect of standing before God and possibly having missed something she should have taught the people. She did note that as a missionary, she would need to learn another language, so she took a course in descriptive linguistics with the Summer Institute of Linguistics at the University of Oklahoma. She had concluded that the Bible was the most important book in the world, and she learned that many people have never had it in their own language. That was it! She would become a Bible translator! At last she felt that she knew the work for which she had been created.

That summer she joined the Bible Translation Organization; several months later she began their jungle camp training in southern Mexico. After all the training she ultimately ended up in the northern Philippines with the Balangao people.

The Balangaos, by tradition, were headhunters. The door had been opened for American Missionaries by American GIs they had met during WW II, and who had treated them with respect.

The job of the Missionary was to learn the Balangao language, put it into written form, and teach the people to read it. The ultimate goal was to give them the Word of God in their own language and teach it to them.

For Jo, being a Missionary was a very new and different experience. Besides the rustic living conditions and the need to adjust to native foods and to a totally new environment, there was the problem of the spirits.

When Jo arrived in Balangao she found that the lives of the people were totally and unmercifully controlled by unusual knowledge of the spirit world and fear of it. They understood the calls of certain birds to be omens. If a man started out to hunt, the call of the omen bird would force him to return home, for it spoke of some danger awaiting him in the forest. They were haunted by their dreams; dreaming of eating meat in certain circumstances meant that someone in the family, usually a child, would surely die. They had to sacrifice a water buffalo in exchange for the child's life. Sacrificing a water buffalo was an expensive endeavor; most families didn't own one. They solicited help from relatives to collect money, but it was so important that no family member would refuse to contribute.

Evil spirits controlled every aspect of their lives. In her book, And the Word Came with Power, written with Patricia Purvis[10] Jo shares a very interesting experience.

I'll never forget the first time Anne and I saw the spirits possess someone. We hadn't been living in Botac long when little Aglipay contracted pneumonia. I'd given him an injection of penicillin, but the spirits, speaking through a medium, told the parents to not allow their son to have another injection. The third day his breathing was labored; it became precariously shallow and slow. He was grasping for air just three or four times a minute. Obviously, he couldn't last much longer. The old spirit medium was called and sacrifices were made. She called the spirits by name to come; she convulsed and shook; then, stiff as a board, she passed out. They caught her as she fell over. People gathered around her, and when she came to, they started asking questions.

"What have we done wrong? What do you want for payment?' 'What do you want for sacrifice?"

Then the woman spoke in a male spirit's voice the spirits simply wanted some pigs and chickens, so they had made the boy sick to get his parents' attention. In exchange for the boy's life, they'd accept three pigs, two chickens, and some rice and wine and beads. The father was immensely relieved; he could meet the spirits' demands.

---

[10] Published and distributed by Wycliffe Bible Translation, Orlando, Florida USA. www.wycliffe.org

The negotiations were finished and with violent wrenching the spirits left the medium. Dazed, she grabbed her sore throat with one hand and her aching head with the other. The man hurried to kill the animals and offer their souls to the spirits. The dying child was well by the next day.

I was dumbfounded. "These spirits really do have power," I thought. It was the spookiest thing I'd ever seen. Small wonder the people argued against following God's way. "If we stop sacrificing, what will we do when our children are sick? Just let them die?"

But there was one person in Bolac who did not sacrifice to the spirits. Only one, Tekla, the only living child of the most powerful spirit medium in all of Balangao, refused to sacrifice. The fascinating story of Tekla and how her experience with the Lord Jesus Christ affected the faith of the Balangao people is also recorded in the book <u>And the Word Came Forth with Power.</u>

Jo, the shy farm girl who grew up in Southern California, was a long way from home. She would spend twenty years with the Balangao people during her 40 year service as a Missionary in the Philippines. It would be necessary for her to make major adjustments. She would have to learn to prepare, digest, and tolerate new foods and rustic accommodations. She would do the work of a midwife, medical specialist, teacher, translator, and counselor.

In her book Joanne speaks about a helicopter accident in which she was involved. Her parents had come from California to visit her. She was going to ride into Balangao in a military helicopter that was taking in building materials to build a clinic. As her father observed men loading more than 10 tons of cement plus other supplies into the Jolly Green Giant, he kept thinking that they were overloading it. She learned later that he wanted to take her off the helicopter, but hesitated. Thirty minutes after they took off, the helicopter crashed. Joanne was buried and other passengers were buried. Fires started where the rotor blades had been. JAARS pilot Bill riding as a guide in the cockpit thrust his arm through the cockpit window, opening the way for them to climb out. The pilot, co-pilot, and crew chief had only minor injuries. When the helicopter pilot shouted. for the people to run because fire threatened an explosion, Bill shouted to the people that Joanne was still inside along with Doming and Dr. Lim. The people threw water and mud from rice fields and put the fires out.

The next day she was airlifted to a United States Air Force base where the young medics worked over her badly marred body, teasing about how good-looking she was. When her parents arrived, her Mom , a nurse with 20 years experience screamed. Joanne looked horrible. The nurses wanted to shave off her cemented hair, her Mom wouldn't let them. She spent the day gently crushing the hunks of blood caked cement out of her hair and then washed it.

The first four days I reasoned with God that I couldn't go blind. I wasn't finished with what he'd sent me to do. When I was able to open my eyes a crack, I could distinguish the light, then shapes appeared. What a relief! I could finish the translation! While buried under the cargo and eyes full of cement, Joanne begged God, reasoning she couldn't go blind; she needed to finish the translation.

Jo finished the translation, and after a time of travel and sharing in the United States, she was back in the Philippines. She subsequently began meeting with church leaders, encouraging them in their walk with the Lord and planning with them how to expedite the fledgling Old Testament translation program. Her excitement and dedication to the work for which God had chosen her is as strong and evident as it ever was.

Jo is awed when after her presentation someone walks up to her and says, "I'm in Missions because of you." Given the opportunity she would tell the world, "Sin is a lot worse than we thought it was. Its consequences are horrible! And it cost God everything. He gave his all! Therefore, our only logical response is to give our all to Him. Don't be afraid to trust God; give Him everything - the end of that is pure joy!"

An Ordinary Woman from England

SUSANNA WESLEY WAS born on January 20th, 1669, the 25th and final child of Dr. Samuel Annesley and Mary White. She died on July 23rd, 1742. She was the mother of John and Charles Wesley. Her father, while at Oxford, became a member of the Church of England and served the parish of Epworth in Lincolnshire for nearly 40 years. John Wesley was born at Epworth, and grew up there. She met Samuel Wesley and was married to him on November 11th, 1688. Samuel and Susanna had nineteen children, but nine died as infants. Only ten of the children lived to maturity.

Susanna was not a preacher. As far as we know, she never preached a sermon, published a book or started a church. But because of her influence on her sons John and Charles Wesley, she is known as the Mother of Methodism.

What John and Charles learned from their mother at home they applied vigorously in their personal lives and in their social lives, as well. They started out simply trying to help people improve their lives. But out of those simple efforts there began to form a movement that would reform the church and society in England. In the early 1700s John, Charles, and a few other students at Oxford University began to meet regularly and devote themselves to a highly disciplined search for holiness and service to others. They fasted until early afternoon on Wednesdays and Fridays, received Holy Communion every week, studied together the Greek New Testament and the Classics, and they visited the sick and imprisoned. They also held each other strictly accountable as Christians. Being very methodical in their devotions; other less disciplined students began to mock them, giving them the name of the "Holy Club", and calling them "Methodists." The Wesley brothers proudly accepted the name, and the eventual result was Methodism.

Formal education was not available to women in 17th century England. The Rev. Dr. Samuel Annesley taught Susanna to read and to think for herself. Dr. Annesley's conscience would not allow him to sign the Act of Uniformity in 1662 that would have meant that he agreed to the changes in the Church of England's Book of Common Prayer. He chose to leave St. Giles Cripplegate in London and founded a new parish. He set an example of independent thinking for his daughter and ultimately for his grandsons, who through their independent thinking, led reform against abuses in church and society.

Samuel and Susanna lived in London and in South Ormsby for a few years and then moved to Epworth, near Lincolnshire. They remained there until he died 40 years later in 1735.

In her lifetime, the Mother of Methodism experienced many hardships. The family was victim of much ridicule! They were targets of various acts of violence because they were known as "dissenters", disagreeing with the King's and the church's politics and failure to care for the needy. Because they were "dissenters", people who opposed them mocked the children, destroyed their crops, and it was suspected that their home was burned because of their beliefs.

Their home was burned down twice. During one of those fires her son John nearly died and had to be rescued from the window of the second floor. He was five years old at the time. The house caught fire during the night, and they thought all of the children had been safely taken out. But when they counted them, John was missing. A neighbor saw little John looking out of an upstairs window in the midst of the leaping flames. Several neighbors climbed on each other's shoulders forming a human ladder until the man on top was able to put his arms around the child and pull him to safety. Just moments later the entire house burst into flames! For the rest of his life John frequently referred to himself as "a brand plucked from the burning." He was quoting from the Bible in Zechariah 3; 2, "Is not this a brand plucked from the fire?" His mother was convinced that little John's life had been spared so that God could use him. Everything had been destroyed in the fire except, according to tradition, part of a page from the Rectory bible. The fragment contained the words "Take up thy cross and follow me." So the Wesley's believed that God had pulled John out of the fire so that he might take up the cross and do God's work.

Susanna's husband was committed to a "debtor's prison" by a parishioner who was demanding payment from him. Samuel left her and the children for over a year because of what amounted to be a minor dispute. It seems that both Susanna and her husband Samuel were strong personalities with strong political and religious opinions. On one occasion royal politics entered their home and caused a separation between Samuel and the family that lasted for about a year.

Susanna was a strong supporter of the Stewart King James who had been overthrown in 1688 and who was replaced by his Dutch Son-in-Law. During a time of family prayers in 1702 Samuel prayed for the new King William, and Susanna refused to say "Amen." Later, John wrote that his mother was "inflexible", and that his father was, as well.

Samuel left home over the incident. His parting words to her were, "Sukey, we must part for if we have two kings we must have two beds." Susanna's response was that she would apologize if she was wrong, but she felt for expediency reconciliation would only be a lie and thus a sin. Several months later and after the death of King William, Samuel returned home, and as a result of their reconciliation, John was born in 1703.

In 1709 a fire quickly destroyed the Epworth Rectory on a cold winter night. Since the family was homeless, they could not remain together. Two daughters stayed with an uncle in London and other children stayed with friends nearby. A month later, when Susanna's 19th child was born, she was thrown into a deep sadness. But she somehow emerged from a state of shock and grief determined to unite her family and to save her children's souls. According to Susanna, surely that was her focus for twenty years of the prime of her life.

Following the rebuilding of the rectory the Matriarch of the Wesley's strictly organized and regulated her home so that she could reassure stability in her family. She wanted to reestablish the need for order and priorities for living a useful life. In the Wesley's home the day began at 5:00am, and specific activities were planned for each hour. Susanna reserved an hour each week for each child inquiring about the state of their soul, their progress, their fears, their expectations, their goals, and their other activities.

Susanna Wesley laid down 16 rules in her home:
1. Eating between meals not allowed.
2. As children they are to be in bed by 8 p.m.
3. They are required to take medicine without complaining.
4. Subdue self-will in a child, and those working together with God to save the child's soul.
5. Teach a child to pray as soon as he can speak.
6. Require all to be still during Family Worship.
7. Give them nothing that they cry for, and only that when asked for politely.
8. Prevent lying, punish no fault which is first confessed and repented of.

9. Never allow a sinful act to go unpunished.
10 Never punish a child twice for a single offense.
11. Comment on and reward good behavior.
12. Any attempt to please, even if poorly performed, should be commended.
13. Preserve property rights, even in smallest matters.
14. Strictly observe all promises.
15. Require no daughter to work before she can read well.
16. Teach children to fear the rod.

Susanna brought up her children in a devout, yet practical way. She chose her methods for rearing and educating her brood from her own experience growing up. Her father had seen the family unit as, as Douglas Graham puts it, a microcosm of the church. He says, "To quote Dr. Annesley's actual words, 'should not families be as well-ordered little commonwealths, well-disciplined Churches?'"

Susanna understood those words to mean that her children should be well disciplined, that they should have a good education, that they should be spiritually mature, and that they should be altruistic.

To accomplish those goals, she believed that it was necessary to break the child's will, or to conquer it as soon as possible, so that they could learn how important it was to obey God's will. She did not mean, however, that she should destroy the children's will-power and force them into a state of fearful submission. As a matter of fact, most of them developed into spirited, strong, self-confident men and women. John was prime proof that her theory worked.

Susanna believed in having a strict systematic routine for eating and sleeping, learning and exercising; spiritual instruction which included prayer and Bible study. As was the practice, she believed in corporal punishment, but she believed in fairness and honesty. No child should be punished twice for the same misdemeanor. While her ideas were far from the modern educational philosophy that encourages total self-expression, Susanna Wesley fostered in her children true independence of thought and action. She had great concern for their physical and moral welfare, but greater concern that they had a true knowledge and commitment to the love of God in Jesus Christ.

Susanna Wesley was a strong Christian woman who was devoted to God and her family. The family was able to survive in the face of grief, hardship and poverty because of her great faith and determination. During the most challenging of times she committed herself to caring for her family the best way she could. With very limited resources, she started a daily school for her children. Although academic education was important, teaching God's word was the most important. She said her most important task was her children's spiritual development and "the saving of their souls." Every day before class she spent an hour in prayer and reading the Bible.

Susanna spent a lot of personal quality time with each of her children which helped them to develop faith, fear of God, and a strong will to survive and succeed. Her effective home schooling caused English society to recognize the importance of education for poor children. At the same time, she influenced the development of trade schools where unskilled people could find a way to move from poverty to a more independent existence. The mother of the Wesley's never emerged as a grand historical or religious figure, but her influence in the lives of her sons John and Charles was decisive in sparking the Methodist movement.

J.B. Wakely, a 19th Century Methodist historian, wrote about Susanna Wesley and the Unauthorized Meetings: While her husband was absent in London in 1711, attending Convocation, Mrs. Wesley adopted the practice of reading to her family and instructing them. One of the servants told his parents and they wished to come. Those told others and they came, until the congregation amounted to forty, and increased till they were over two hundred, and the parsonage could not contain all that came. She read to them the best and most awakening sermons she could find in the library, talked to the people freely and affectionately. Their meetings were held "because she thought that the end of the institution of the Sabbath was not fully answered by attending the Church unless the intermediate spaces of time were filled up by other acts of devotion."

Inman, the Curate, was a very stupid and narrow man. He became jealous because her audience was larger than his, and he wrote to Mr. Wesley, complaining that his wife, in his absence, had turned the parsonage into a conventicle, that the Church was likely to be scandalized by such irregular proceedings and that they ought to be tolerated no longer. Mr. Wesley wrote to his wife that she should get someone else to read the sermons. She replied that there was not a man there that could read a sermon without spoiling it.

Inman still complained, and the Rector wrote to Mrs. Wesley that the meetings should be discontinued. Mrs. Wesley answered him by showing what good the meetings had done and that none were opposed to them but Mr. Inman and one other. She then concludes with these wonderful sentences: "If after all this you think fit to dissolve this assembly do not tell me you desire me to do it, for that will not satisfy my conscience, but send your positive command in such full and express terms as may absolve me from all guilt and punishment for neglecting this opportunity for doing good when you and I shall appear before the great and awful tribunal of our Lord Jesus Christ."

Were not these the first Methodist meetings held by the Wesley's?

Can we wonder that Isaac Taylor says that "the mother of the Wesley's was the mother of Methodism; and that in her characteristic letter, when she said, '"Do not advise me, but command me to desist,'" she was bringing to its place a corner-stone of the future of Methodism. "Who can tell the influence that those meetings of their mother in the parsonage had upon John and Charles in future years, who were then little boys, and always present!"

About 300 years ago, response to the criticism that he was not staying within parish boundaries or in church but preaching the gospel to anyone, anywhere who would listen John Wesley wrote, "The world is my parish." Today there are about 18 million Methodist Christians in the world, twelve million are United Methodists, and the other 6 million belong to the other 22 branches of Methodism.

"Help me, Lord, to remember that religion is not to be confined to the church...nor exercised only in prayer and meditation, but that everywhere I am in thy presence. Whatever weakens your reason, whatever impairs the tenderness of your conscience, whatever obscures your sense of God, whatever increases the authority of your body over your mind, whatever takes away from your relish for spiritual things, that to you is sin, no matter how innocent it is in itself. May I be careful to have my mind in order when I take upon myself the honor to speak to the sovereign Lord of the universe, remembering that upon the temper of my soul depends, in very great measure, my success." Susanna, Mother of the Wesley's.

Jesus

NOW I WANT you to meet a very special friend. In fact, He is much more than a friend. We know about Jesus from various sources such as secular history, art and literature, from the Holy Bible, from hymns and spiritual songs and also personal experiences.

Christianity as a religion came from Judaism, but as a Community of Faith it owes its existence to Jesus Christ. After several centuries of development through lawgivers, priests and prophets, Judaism had become the major religion of Israel. Religions and political conflicts had caused a division in the nation of Israel into two distinct kingdoms, one to the north, and the other to the south. Both kingdoms were conquered by aggressors from the Tigress-Euphrates valley. In the meantime, many of the people, including many important leaders, were deported, and only a small group, a remnant remained.

It was through the good will of Persian kings like Cyrus that Palestine became included within their boundaries, and a new temple was built in Jerusalem. The Temple became the center for the remnant as well as for those who had been scattered in the dispersion.

The term Jew refers to a person whose religion is Judaism. In broader terms a Jew is a member of a world-wide cultural group that traditionally practices the Jewish religion. The word itself comes from the Hebrew Yehudi, the Latin Judaeus, and originally meant "belonging to the tribe of Judah." Judah was one of the twelve tribes of Israel, descended from Judah who was the fourth son of Jacob.[11]

After their escape from Egypt the tribe of Judah entered Canaan and settled in the region south of Jerusalem. In time Judah became the strongest and most influential tribe,

---

[11] *Genesis 29:35 New Living Translation*

producing two great kings; David and his son Solomon. It was prophesied that the Messiah would come from Judah." Messenger of good news; Shout to Zion from the mountaintop! Shout louder to Jerusalem -do not be afraid. Tell the towns of Judah; Your God is coming!" Yes, the sovereign Lord is coming in all his glorious power. He will rule with awesome strength. See, he brings his reward with him as he comes. He will feed his flock like a shepherd. He will carry the lambs in his arms, holding them close to his heart. He will gently lead the mother sheep with their young[12]."

The Jews as a people were held together by the religion of Judaism which was strengthened by persecution. Antiochus Epiphanes tried to force Greek culture on the Jews, but they revolted under the leadership of the Maccabees.

I don't think we hear much about the Maccabees nowadays in Protestant circles, but we do hear about Hanukkah, or the Festival of Lights. It begins on the 25th day of the Jewish calendar month of Kislev and lasts for eight days and nights. It begins at sundown with blessings, games, and special festive foods. During Hanukkah Jewish people celebrate the religious and military triumphs of ancient Jewish heroes.

About 2,200 years ago the Greek-Syrian ruler Antioch IV attempted to force Greek culture on peoples in his territory. Jews who lived in Judea, which is now Israel were not allowed to practice their religion or study the Torah. Although they were greatly outnumbered, religious Jews in the region armed themselves and fought to protect themselves and their religion. They were led by Mattathias, the Hasmonean, and later by his son Judah, the Maccabee. The rebelling army became known as the Maccabees.

The Maccabees fought for three years, and in 3597, or about 165 B.C.E. they victoriously reclaimed the Temple on Jerusalem's Mount Moriah. Following their victory, they prepared the Temple for rededication. In Hebrew the word

---

[12] *Isaiah 40:9-11,* New International Translation)

Hanukkah means "dedication." But when they entered the Temple, they found only enough purified oil to keep the Temple light burning for a single day, but there was a miracle. The light continued to burn for eight days.

The lighting of the Menorah is known in Hebrew as the hanukiya and is the most important Hanukkah tradition. The Menorah is the candle stand with nine branches. There are usually eight candles all of the same height with a taller candle in the middle, called the Shamash or the "servant" which is used to light the others. Every evening of Hanukkah one more candle is lit along with a special blessing.

The Menorah symbolizes the burning light in the Temple, and marks the eight days of the Hanukkah festival. Some say that it also celebrates the light of freedom which was won by the Maccabees for the Jewish people.

The Dreidel has been a favorite Hanukkah toy for a long time. However, it once had a serious purpose. When the Syrians forbid study of the Torah, Jews who studied in secret kept spinning tops "suivons, or dreidels" on hand so that if they were found studying, they could quickly pretend that they were only playing. Outside of Israel, a dreidel contains the Hebrew letters "nun" and "gimel" "hay" and "shin." That means, "A great miracle happened here." Those Hebrew letters also represent Yiddish words that explain how to play the dreidel game. In the beginning each player has the same amount of candies, chocolate coins (gelt), or other tokens, and puts one in a pot. Each player takes a turn spinning the dreidel, waiting to see which letter lands face up. Nun means "nisht:" do nothing. Gimel "gants" says take the pot. Hay is for "halb." Shin is for "shtel." That means add to the pot. The game ends when one person wins all of the tokens[13].

After the Maccabean victory the people established a small state where the High Priest was the central figure. Rome, which was becoming bigger and more powerful, incorporated the Jewish state within its boundaries. Herod, who was not a

---

[13] Thanks to Holly Hartman for the information gathered on the Hanukkah.

Jew, married into the Maccabees family and with consent from Rome became the political ruler over the small state and rebuilt the Temple in

Jerusalem. The Maccabees had dreams of a community where God's will, as expressed in the Jewish Law and the Prophets, would be observed, a religious state. But with the coming of Herod on the scene, the dream was broken. Instead, the Jewish state came under the government of a foreign ruler whose main ambition was to establish his own dynasty. However, it was during the reign of Herod that Jesus Christ was born.

My friend Jesus was of humble birth, but his coming had been predicted in the Hebrew Bible, called by Christians the Old Testament. Jewish people had been expecting the coming of a Messiah to help them shake off the yoke of Roman oppression. Various scriptures pointed to Jesus of Nazareth as that anticipated Savior. I have always been inspired by traditional hymns. The following Gospel hymn is one of my favorites;[14]

More about Jesus I would know, More of His grace to others show;
More of His saving fullness see, More of His love who died for me.
More about Jesus let me learn, More of His holy will discern;
Spirit of God, my teacher be, showing the things of Christ to me.
More about Jesus in His word, Holding communion with my Lord;
Hearing His voice in ev'ry line, making each faithful saying mine.
More about Jesus on His throne, Riches in glory all His own;
More of His kingdom's sure increase; More of His coming,

---

[14] *More About Jesus* was written in 1887; the words by E.E. Hewitt, and the tune by John R. Sweeney

Prince of Peace.
More, more about Jesus, More, more about Jesus;
More of His saving fullness see, More of His love who died for me.

So, let's learn more about Jesus. The words Christian and Christianity come to us from the word **Christ** or **Messiah** meaning **Anointed one.** Very early in history the Jews were preparing for the coming of the Christ. In the New Testament we read, "But when the right time came, God sent his Son, born of a woman, subject to the law. God sent him to buy freedom for us who were slaves to the law, so that he could adopt us as his very own children. And because you Gentiles have become his children, God has sent the spirit of his Son into your hearts, and now you can call him God, your dear Father. Now you are no longer a slave, but God's own child. And since you are his child, everything he has belongs to you[15]." Those comforting words give us the assurance that as Christians we are God's chosen people, and that we have full rights as children of God.

In four different books of the New Testament, named after their writers we can find the record of Jesus' life. As you read the Gospels you will discover that Matthew, Mark, Luke, and John are the principal sources for the Christian biography of Jesus as the Son of God. Matthew, Mark, and Luke are referred to by biblical scholars as synoptic because they are very similar in content, language, and structure. Each of the synoptic Gospels tells the story of Jesus and proclaims him as the Son of God, the Son of Man, the Messiah, and the Judge, according to the book of Revelation. The Gospel of John emphasizes the deity of Jesus Christ. It is the only Gospel where Jesus talks with a person of Jewish authority, Nicodemus on the need to be born again, emphasizing the importance of a spiritual rebirth, saying that people could not enter the Kingdom of Heaven by living a better life, but by being spiritually reborn.

---

[15]Galatians 4;4-7(The New Living Translation)

If you were to travel throughout this country asking people to tell you what their religion was you would probably get answers such as Protestant, Jewish, agnostic, Catholic, Muslim, or atheist etc. But if you were to ask a more specific question, such as, "Are you a Christian?" what kind of answers would you expect? Since I have been a United Methodist Pastor for the past thirty years, I have asked that question many times. One lady told me that she was a Catholic, and after a brief pause she said, "yes." One older stately gentleman proudly answered my question by saying, "I'm a Presbyterian." As I recall, he spoke with a heavy Scottish accent. One lady told me proudly that she had been a member of the First Baptist Church for more than fifty years and that she had served in various leadership capacities within that church. One well-groomed gentleman said, "Why of course! I'm a thirty-second degree Mason!" A friend said, "I believe in God. I try to be a Christian, I hope I am." One man told me that he did not want to call himself a Christian because he thought it made him sound conceited.

I have heard people who have been church members for many years say that they didn't know if they were Christians or not. Of course there were some who said that they were definitely not Christians, and others who said that they didn't even believe in God.

So what is a Christian? According to the New Testament[16], the believers in Christ were first called Christians in Antioch, an ancient city on the eastern side of the Orontes River. Antioch is located near the modern city of Antakya, Turkey. The church at Antioch was a mixture of Jews who spoke Greek or Aramaic, and Gentiles. They were of different cultures, races, and languages. What they had in common was Christ. Therefore, the people around them called them "Christ Ones." Through the years and centuries, the love of Christ has crossed boundaries and united peoples of all languages, races and cultures.

---

[16] Acts 11:26 And when he had found him, he brought him unto Antioch. And it came to pass, that a whole year they assembled themselves with the church, and taught much people. And the disciples were called Christians first in Antioch.

How is it that one becomes a Christian? Phrases such as being saved, being converted, being changed, accepting Christ, being born again, asking Jesus to come into your heart have similar meanings. All of those expressions refer to the experience of becoming a Christian.

Some very sincere, deep-thinking people have quite a struggle defining themselves as Christians. It might be because they don't know what a Christian actually is. Maybe they don't understand that to be a Christian does not mean to have a religion, but to have a relationship. Some people believe that it is simply too difficult, and that despite their best efforts, they can never be good enough to deserve salvation. If that is what they believe, they have a good point, and they are thinking in the right direction. Here is where the Bible offers some very helpful insights. In Ephesians 2:8-10[17], we read, "For by grace you have been saved through faith; and that is not your own doing; it is the gift of God, not because of works, lest any man should boast. For we are his workmanship created in Christ Jesus for good works, which God prepared beforehand, that we should walk in them." The New Living Translation might be easier to understand. It says, "God saved you by his special favor when you believed. And you can't take credit for this; it is a gift from God. Salvation is not a reward for the good things we have done, so none of us can boast about it. For we are God's masterpiece. He created us anew in Christ Jesus so that we can do the good things he planned for us long ago." It is not as a result of any effort, ability, skill, craft or intelligent choice or act of service that we become Christians. It is through God's unmerited favor, or grace that we are saved. God intends for us to live out our Christian lives in acts of service since we are not saved merely for our own benefit, but to make disciples for Christ and to strengthen his church.

But what is the process? How, and at what point does one actually become a Christian? There are some things about which we are pretty certain. We are born, we interact with the world around us; we pay taxes, and we die. There are also

---

[17] Revised Standard Version

some important aspects of our existence about which we are not so sure. We don't know how long we will live. We don't know how we will impact the world around us, and most people don't have any idea what will happen to them after they die.

Campus Crusade for Christ, an international organization that promotes Christian evangelism and discipleship in over 190 countries, is probably the largest evangelical organization in the United States. It was established by Bill Bright in 1951 at the University of California at Los Angeles, primarily as a ministry to college students, but has since been expanded to include outreach to professional adults, high school students, athletes, and entire families. Campus Crusade for Christ is the publisher of a very popular and effective Christian Gospel message called *The Four Spiritual Laws.*

Just as there are physical laws that govern the physical universe, so are there spiritual laws which govern your relationship with God.

The first law is that God loves you and offers a wonderful plan for your life.
God's Love
"...God so loved the world that He gave His only Son, that whoever believes in Him shall not perish, but have eternal life.[18]"
God's Plan
Jesus said, "I came that they might have life, and might have it abundantly" that it might be full and meaningful[19].

The Second Law is that man is sinful and separated from God. Therefore, he cannot know and experience God's love and plan for his life.

Man is sinful

---

[18] John 3:16 NIV
[19] John 10:10

"All have sinned and fall short of the glory of God[20]." Man was created to have fellowship with God; but, because of his stubborn self-will, characterized by an attitude of active rebellion and passive indifference, he commits what the Bible calls sin.

Man is separated
"The wages of sin is death[21] "(spiritual separation from God)
Since God is holy, and human beings are sinful a great gulf separates the two. Humans are continually trying to reach God and the abundant life through their own efforts, such as a good life, philosophy, or religion—but they inevitably fail.

The third law explains the only way to bridge the gulf. It says that Jesus Christ is the only provision for man's sin. Through Him you can know and experience God's love and plan for your life.

He died in our place.
God demonstrates His own love toward us, in that while we were yet sinners, Christ died for us[22]"

He rose from the dead.
"Christ died for our sins—was buried—He was raised on the third day, according to the scriptures. He appeared to Peter, then to the twelve. After that He appeared to more than five hundred[23]

He is the only way to God.
"Jesus said to him, 'I am the way, the truth, and the life; no one comes to the Father, but through me[24]."

---

[20] Romans 3:23
[21] Romans 6:23
[22] Romans 5:8
[23] 1st Corinthians 15;3-6
[24] John 14;6

God has bridged the gulf which separates us from Him by sending His Son, Jesus Christ to die on the cross in our place to pay the penalty for our sins.

Since it is not enough just to know those three laws, the fourth spiritual law says that we must individually receive Jesus Christ as Savior and Lord, then we can know the experience of God's love and plan for our lives.

We must receive Christ.
"As many as received Him, to them He gave the right to become children of God, even those who believe in His name[25]."

We receive Christ through faith
"By grace you have been saved through faith, and that not of yourselves, it is the gift of God; not as a result of works, that no one should boast[26]."

When we receive Christ, we experience a New Birth[27]

We receive Christ by personal invitation.
Jesus said, "Behold, I stand at the door and knock; if anyone hears my voice, and opens the door, I will come in to him[28]."

Receiving Christ involves turning to God from self (repentance) and trusting Christ to come into our lives, to forgive our sins, and to make us what He wants us to be. Just to agree intellectually that Jesus Christ is the Son of God, and that He died on the cross for our sins is not enough. Neither is it enough to have an emotional experience. We receive Jesus Christ by faith, an act of the will. There are basically two kinds of life situations, the self-directed life, and the Christ-directed life.

---

[25] John 1:12
[26] Ephesians 2;8-9
[27] Read John 3;1-8 for details
[28] Revelation 3:20

In the **SELF-DIRECTED LIFE**
The self is on the throne. Interests are directed by self, resulting in discord and frustration.

In the **CHRIST- DIRECTED LIFE**
Christ is on the throne. Self is yielding to Christ. Interests are directed by Christ, resulting in harmony with God's plan.

The question is, is yours a Self- Directed life or a Christ-Directed life? What kind of life do you desire?

You can receive Christ right now by faith through prayer. Prayer is talking and listening to God.

YOU SHOULD UNDERSTAND that God knows your heart, and is not so concerned with your words as He is with the attitude of your heart. Here is a suggestion for a prayer.

> "Lord Jesus, I need you. Thank you for dying on the cross for my sins. I open the door of my life and receive You as my Savior and Lord. Thank you for forgiving my sins and giving me eternal life. Take control of the throne of my life. Make me the kind of person you want me to be. Amen."

I HAVE INCLUDED the information about the Four Spiritual Laws, hoping that they will be helpful to anyone who is in search of a right relationship with God. As it was stated above, when a person makes a decision to accept Christ as his or her Savior, the words are not as important as the attitude.

Following is another prayer that one might consider praying:

> "Heavenly Father, I know that I have broken your rules and because of my sins I am separated from you, and I am truly sorry. I believe that your Son, Jesus Christ, died for my sins, has risen from the dead, and hears my prayer right now. I invite Jesus to become my Lord and Savior

and to rule and reign in my heart from now on. God, help me to turn away from my sinful ways and follow you. Lord hear my prayer, in Jesus' name. Amen. "

My prayer was the following:
"Lord Jesus Christ, I know I'm a sinner and that I don't deserve to go to Heaven. I don't deserve your blessings. But I believe that you died on that cross for my sins. Please come into my heart and my life and save me. Please forgive my sins, and when I die, take me to heaven to be with you. Amen."

It was not a long prayer, but it came straight from the bottom of my heart, and I knew immediately that Jesus answered me. I felt a great relief; a tremendous load was lifted from me. As John Wesley said, "I knew that Christ had taken away my sins!"

But that is just the beginning. After accepting Christ, if you have not been baptized, that is the next step. If you have received Christian baptism, a second baptism is not necessary. What is necessary is church attendance and membership, daily prayer and bible study. You are now what some people refer to as a "born again" Christian, which simply means a Christian in the biblical sense. There was a powerful Jewish leader who came to Jesus one night and questioned him. Jesus told him that in order to even see the kingdom of heaven he had to be "born again", or born from above," not in a physical sense, but in a spiritual sense.

Once that happens, you are in a unique position to be used by God. God can use you in many ways. Three of those was are, serving, sharing your faith, and living by the Spirit. Serving is letting yourself be used to work for good wherever you are needed. You can do whatever you are able, especially what you do best. But it is not necessary to be an expert at the job you are doing. You just need to be willing to serve.

I remember hearing one of the pastors in a United Methodist church in New Jersey a few years ago talking about Bishop Dale White. He said that once at a church dinner after everyone had finished eating and people were just milling around, the Bishop did something that he thought was unusual. He put on an apron and began cleaning the tables. That was clearly not the Bishop's area of expertise, but he saw the need and the opportunity to serve, and he began to serve. John Wesley said, "Do all the good you can, by all the means you can, in all the ways you can, in all the places you can at all the times you can, to all the people you can, as long as ever you can.!" The apostle Paul said, "Whenever we have the opportunity we should do good to everyone, especially to our Christian brothers and sisters[29]."

Don't be afraid to talk about Jesus. You don't have to be an evangelist in order to share your faith. Just tell about how God has been real in your life. A well-known gospel hymn says "--- I love to tell the story, for some have never heard the message of salvation from God's own holy word." You don't have to preach in order to tell someone about Christ. All you have to do is speak honestly from your personal experience. It is true that some people, in fact many people have never heard a live personal witness from a sincere dedicated Christian. Did God answer your prayers? You can share that! Do you know Christ as your Lord and Savior? Many people need and want to hear that! Are your habits and thoughts and decisions based on Christian principles? You can tell that! Do you have a Christian routine in your life, and does it work? Surely you can share that! Are there special moments in your life when Jesus speaks to you and lifts you up? There are many who have never heard of such blessings. But you can be a blessing if you are willing to share. In recent years I have told people about how faith in God through Christ has caused major changes in my life.

Some had never known that Christ could take away negative life-threatening habits. Some have never known that Jesus Christ could take away bitter racial hatred for good. Some have never known that they could know the Lord in a

---

[29] *(Galatians 6;10,N.L.T. Bible)*

personal way! God can and will use you if you are willing to share your faith. In order to live by the Spirit, we have to be obedient to God and let God guide our entire life. That means we have to be open to the Holy Spirit all day, every day. According to the Wikipedia Free Encyclopedia, The New England Primer was the first reader designed for the American Colonies, and became the most successful colonial educational textbook. I had no clue that it was the source of my first bed time prayer:

Now I lay me down to sleep, I pray the Lord my soul to keep;
If I should die before I wake, I pray the Lord my soul to take.

A more hopeful version of the same prayer is;
Now I lay me down to sleep,
I pray the Lord my soul to keep;
Guide us through the starry night,
And wake us in the morning light.
I ask not for myself alone, but for thy children-everyone

At the open and the close of each day God must have complete control.

Ruben P. Job wrote and compiled a small devotional resource called Three Simple Rules, *A Wesleyan Way of Living.* Onenyear, I received a copy as a gift from my District Superintendent. It contains three prayers that I suggest are highly appropriate to be prayed by anyone who wants to live by the Spirit.

The first is to be prayed at the beginning of the day {Inviting God's Intervention in Our Lives}:

Loving Teacher, come and make your home in our hearts this day, Dwell within us all day long and save us from error or foolish ways. Teach us today to do no harm, to do good, and assist us so that we stay in loving relationship with you and our neighbor. Help us today to be an answer to another's prayer so that we may be one of your signs of hope in the world you love.

The second prayer is to be prayed at Midday and is for welcoming God's Presence:

> God of love, holiness, and strength, we thank you for the gift of your presence through the morning hours. Continue to make yourself and your way known to us throughout the remaining hours of the day. Grant us grace to follow you in faithfulness, joy and peace. We are yours.

And the third prayer is to be prayed at the End of the Day:

> Tender shepherd of my soul; make yourself and your way known to me in this evening time of prayer and reflection. Bring awareness of my failures and confidence in your desire and ability to forgive my sins, heal my wounds, and mend my broken places. By the power of your presence bring me to the end of the day whole, complete, and at peace with you, my neighbor and myself. Grant a night of peaceful rest, and send me forth tomorrow as a witness to your love and grace.

I am very grateful to Debbie Heisley-Cato for that resource that for the past year has become a part of my daily devotions.

As you recall, this book is about how God uses ordinary people. Are you an ordinary person? Perhaps you are ordinary in some ways and extraordinary *in* other ways. That is your call; you decide. Just let God use you.

I WILL LEAVE you with a prayer that I wrote and start my every morning with. It is called "Prayer Warrior's Morning Prayer."

> Heavenly Father,
> I thank you for the rest, protection, provisions, and peace that you have provided for me throughout the night. I thank you God for another day that I have never seen before. Lord, I recognize this day as a day of responsibilities, and a day of infinite

possibilities. Please forgive all my sins, and guide my words, my steps, and my actions this day so that they may be in accordance with your will. Show me today what I can have, and what I need to leave alone. Please keep my mind alert, and my body strong. Guide my steps by your word so that I will not be overcome by any evil. Lord, help me to not waste any time, money, or space this day, but to make the best use of those gifts that you have given to all of us. May I have at least one opportunity to do good this day. May my thoughts, words, and actions be motivated by love. Let me take the time to think about the goodness of the Lord in the land of the living, and especially in my life. Let me Praise God today with my heart and my voice. Protect and guide all true Prayer Warriors by your Spirit. Lord, help me to do all that I can to be at peace with my neighbors, my family and my friends. Help me, when I pause for evening rest, to remember a good deed I have done, and to be thankful. Let there be peace especially in my home. Please let no circumstance, situation, attitude, thing or person keep me from praying every day. Let me never forget that "Greater is He that is in me than he that is in the world." God I know that you hear me, and I expect a blessing today. Help me to keep my Bible with me and to take time to read it every day. I ask these things in the precious name of Jesus Christ our Lord, and to Him be all power and glory forever and ever.

Amen

Resources

http://gbgm-umc.org/umw/Wesley/
http://www.susanpellowe.com/sw/io.html, Heather Graham
http://ChristianityTodayLibrary.com
http://wwwctlibrary.com/ch/1982issue2/216.html
The Mother's Heart Magazine (www.The-Mothers-Heart.com),
The Board of Global Ministries of The United Methodist Church, (Ronald M. Higashi) History's women (http://www.historys-women.com/womenoffaith/SusannahWesley.html),

Susannah, Mother of The Wesley's (Abingdon), and http://en.wikipedia.org/wiki/Susanna Wesley", John Wesley: Holiness of Heart and Life

https://en.wikipedia.org/wiki/Jim_Crow_laws
https://en.wikipedia.org/wiki/Boxer_Rebellion
http://www.lincoln.ed/about/history

New International Version (NIV) Holy Bible, New International Version®, NIV® Copyright ©1973, 1978, 1984, 2011 by Biblica, Inc. ® Used by permission. All rights reserved worldwide.

New Living Translation (NLT) Holy Bible, New Living Translation, copyright © 1996, 2004, 2015 by Tyndale House Foundation. Used by permission of Tyndale House Publishers Inc., Carol Stream, Illinois 60188. All rights reserved.

Revised Standard Version (RSV) Revised Standard Version of the Bible, copyright © 1946, 1952, and 1971 the Division of Christian Education of the National Council of the Churches of Christ in the United States of America. Used by permission. All rights reserved

King James Version (KJV) Public Domain